THE
missing pages
OF THE PARENT HANDBOOK

christina brockett

Stella Maris
PRESS

International Standard Book Number: 978-0-9889379-1-8

Library of Congress Catalog Card Number: 2013937787

Printed in the United States of America

In order to protect their privacy, the names of some individuals cited in this book have been changed. Any similarities to real names of persons are purely coincidental.

NOTE: This publication contains the opinions and ideas of its author and contributors. It is intended to provide helpful and informative material on the subject matter covered. It is sold with the understanding that the author, contributors and publisher are not engaged in rendering professional services in the book. If the reader requires personal assistance or advice, a competent professional should be consulted.

The author, contributors and publisher specifically disclaim any responsibility for any liability, loss, or risk, personal or otherwise, which is incurred as a consequence, directly or indirectly, of the use and application of any of the contents of this book.

Design: Lookout Design, Inc.
www.lookoutdesign.com

Editorial development and creative design support by Ascent:
www.itsyourlifebethere.com

For my two monkeys

Contents

Introduction

AS A WORKING MOTHER of a boy and girl, ages ten and seven, I have had moments where I felt completely unprepared to be a parent—where I was overcome by dread that took residence in the pit of my stomach. It's that feeling you get when you walk into a classroom and realize that your exam was today, and you haven't even opened the book. Or you skipped class, or were asleep when they covered some key item you needed to be successful.

I still have those moments.

Before my children were born, I was an executive with a big international company managing a team of individuals working large-scale projects. I was hired based on my skill, qualifications, and ability to get the job done. Later I changed jobs, again hired for my expertise. Then I became a parent, perhaps the biggest job of my life, and I felt, and at times still feel, utterly unqualified.

Whether it is an issue concerning my children's health, education, or simple emotional well-being, I am sometimes astounded by the fact that these little people are wholly dependent on me to get it right. Over the years, I have attacked the idea of parenthood just like any other subject that I needed to learn by reading books, magazines, etc. Yet with all of that, there are still times when I feel I have overestimated my ability to be a good parent.

I distinctly remember one night when my son CJ was just a toddler. His fever had spiked, leaving him listless with full, pink cheeks and glazed eyes. The night had been a long one, which had left both my husband and me exhausted. While my husband attempted to get some sleep, I put my son in the bathtub in an effort to bring his temperature down. Gently pouring the lukewarm water over his body, I offered CJ what seemed like hollow assurances and realized I was clueless and really had very little idea of what I was doing.

CJ's fever broke later that night and he was back to normal within another two days, but I wasn't. Shortly after this incident, I shared my feelings of inadequacy over coffee with a friend of mine, a mother of four. As I talked to her it became apparent I wasn't alone—that we have all had times when we were frustrated that we didn't have the answers or the ultimate guide on how to parent.

As an outlet for my feelings, I began to write essays on my parenting experiences and started sharing these with other parents I knew. In turn, they began to share their stories and words of wisdom with me. Through these conversations, I felt as if I were beginning to fill in some of the pages missing from my parent handbook. In speaking with them, I realized that although each child and experience is different, shaped by both who we are as parents and by each child's uniqueness, there are common "lessons learned" that could and *should* be shared.

What began as casual conversations with a few friends turned into a two-year ongoing quest to interview parents from all over the country about their experiences in the parental trenches. Some of the interviews were one-on-ones and others took place in group settings where friends, and friends of friends, gathered to meet with me to share their "oh crap" moments when parenting dealt them a situation in which they felt wholly unprepared.

The result is a collection of stories based on the shared experiences, insights, wisdom, and hard-won lessons gained from moments when our parenting skills ran out. In those moments, each of us whose stories appear here was certain we had been given the one edition of *The Parent Handbook* from which a key page was missing.

Let me be clear. This is not a guidebook or a counseling handbook. None of us whose experiences are captured here is a child-rearing expert. In each story, I have tried to capture the essence of the experience, while filling in descriptive details as necessary. At the request of some parents, I have altered some names and other identifying details. But we offer our brief stories in the hopes that you can grow more confident, more wise and caring, in this complex business of parenting.

So, if you are like us—normal parents who love our children but sometimes feel inadequate or unprepared for the challenges of raising a child—welcome!

We want to offer you our tough, scary, overwhelming, sometimes humorous and often perplexing experiences, as well as the lessons learned from them. In this book, we hope you will find at least some of those missing pages that were left out of your handbook, too.

Confronting Fear

Tina's Missing Pages: When you don't know what your child really needs—motivation or a break

CJ STOOD STIFF AS A SENTRY, his hands clenched around his goggles. A nervous smile stretched across his face. I pulled him toward me, and we sat down on the bench near another mother and her son. In a few minutes the swim team tryouts would begin. I began the idle small talk, obligatory in these situations. The conversation covered your basics: comments on the coolness of the weather that morning; where you lived; previous swimming experience; and any possible connections between people you knew. It was that awkward exchanging of pleasantries where you are equally aware that you, as well as your child, are being "sized up." Beneath these surface pleasantries, I tried to mask my anxiety for my seven-year-old son, who I knew was a nervous wreck.

A month before, CJ and his friends Chris and Ryan were

sitting around on a Friday afternoon when they began talking about how excited they were for the end of school and for the upcoming swim team year. Both Chris and Ryan had been on the team the two prior years; CJ had not. CJ, historically terrified of the water, had preferred instead to watch from the sidelines. Therefore, I was a little surprised when CJ approached me about trying out with the other boys.

That Friday afternoon, after closing the door behind his friends, CJ slid onto a stool near where I was cooking and said, "Mom, I think this year I want to try out for the swim team."

His desire to go beyond the sidelines was huge, but I also knew that despite his skill, sometimes his fears paralyzed him. Historically when this has happened, it has hampered his progress—much more so than had he not tried at all. If he succeeded, then his confidence would get a huge boost and he would continue to make positive strides forward. If he failed, he would take more than one step back. This time I knew he would inevitably compare himself to his friends, their ease of success magnifying his failure.

I smiled at him. All I could do in that moment was support his decision to try.

"Sweetie, I think that's awesome. You've worked really hard swimming this past year and are now a much stronger swimmer. If you want to do this, we'll make it happen. But you need to be aware that the swim team practices and meets are often early in the morning. Are you good with that?"

"Yeah, I'm good. It'll be fun just to hang out with the guys."

Now here we were, waiting for the tryouts to start. I knew things could go either way, and I had no idea how I was going to handle it if he panicked. This was going to be a tremendous balancing act, and I didn't know if I had what it took to do it well.

The minutes passed and CJ stood there, like many of the swimmers, adjusting his goggles and shifting his weight back and forth between his feet. There was no indication there would be an issue, just the air of nervous anticipation among CJ and the other swimmers.

The sparkling cobalt pool, divided by strings of red, white, and blue plastic floats, was waiting. The testing lane lay underneath a large pine tree, its bows undulating in the chlorine-laced breeze, causing the lane to appear occasionally darker and more foreboding.

For some here, the sight and smell of the pool seemed to evoke a sense of nostalgia, and there was an exchange of knowing smiles amid the other parents. However, my stomach tensed and I silently said a little prayer. I saw the clock through the sea of brightly colored bathing suits littering the concrete decking. It was time.

A parade of young swim coaches in their Aéropostale shirts and long shorts walked past with their clipboards and signaled for us to follow. Slowly we walked over to the far side of the pool and waited patiently for their direction.

When they asked who wanted to volunteer to be tested first, CJ looked at me and smiled, as if seeking my approval. I smiled in return, supporting whatever decision he wanted to make. The next thing I knew, a boy slightly older than mine was in the pool. As he dipped his toes in the water, a grimace appeared and he quickly withdrew them. Clearly, the water was cold, which didn't surprise me. Unseasonably cold for June, the temperatures that day had reached only seventy-three degrees. At the encouragement of his mother, the other boy got back into the water. After quickly adjusting his goggles, he was swimming, stroke after stroke, until he reached the end.

My body relaxed slightly at the boy's accomplishment. Knowing that CJ had seen the boy succeed, I hoped that it might remove any apprehension that he had. CJ stood, his ill-fitting bathing suit barely covering his angular hip bones. Turning, he grinned at me and pulled down his goggles.

"I'm ready, Mom," he said with utter confidence, and signaled to the coach that he wanted to go next.

I walked behind him as he approached the pool. Reaching the edge, CJ noticed for the first time that he was getting in at the twelve-foot mark. Although he had swum all winter, the full length and back of a regulation pool, it had been only six feet at its deepest point. He couldn't stand at six feet, just as he couldn't stand at twelve feet; the difference was that he had never entered a pool this deep. I prayed that it wouldn't be a problem. CJ turned around and looked at me, his muscles tensing in his jaw and arms. Familiar with the self-doubt I was seeing in his eyes, I stepped toward him, put my hand on his shoulder, and gave it a gentle squeeze.

"I'll be by your side the whole way. You can do this, CJ. I've *seen* you do it."

A few seconds later, he submerged his body and took two strokes. Then he turned toward the side of the pool and swam toward the edge where I was standing. He pulled himself out and, turning away from the crowd, yanked his goggles off to reveal his contorted face and his eyes filling up with tears.

"I can't do it. I just can't. It's too deep, Mommy. It's too cold. I can't do it."

My heart ached for him as I wrapped a towel around his tiny shoulders and drew him to me, away from the watchful eyes of the other kids and their parents—as much for his sake as well as for my own.

As I cradled him in my arms, my heart raced in my chest. Instinctually I knew that if I didn't get my son back in the water to at least try, he would forever convince himself that he was incapable of swimming on a team like his friends. Frankly, I didn't care whether CJ was on the team; I only wanted him to have fun and become a stronger swimmer. Having witnessed him swim all winter, I took a mental inventory. Could he physically do this? Yes. Was his difficulty more mental, combined with the cold? I thought so. Glancing at the clock, I knew the evaluations were coming to a close.

I pushed CJ away from me, my hands still planted on his shoulders. I said, "Look at me, honey; you *can* do this. You swam all winter, the *full* length of the pool and back. I know it's a little cold—okay, maybe a lot cold—but all you need to do is try."

Tears welled up in his eyes. His choked response: "I just can't, Mom."

My heart raced with my mind. Embracing him, I wished I could absorb all of his stress and fear into my body, and infuse confidence in return, but I knew I had a job to do as a parent—although I wasn't entirely confident I knew what the real issue was. Should I encourage him to surrender to his fear, or to face it head-on? What if his gut sense was right and he genuinely couldn't do this? If I pushed him on and he failed, he would be humiliated. There was also the possibility that he could panic and have his fear of water reinstated, or even worse potentially drown. Or did he actually need me to be his voice of confidence? And just how could I do that when I was not confident that I knew what he truly needed right then?

I separated from CJ and looked at him. His eyes met mine, and I searched them for answers. "Do you really believe after all of your hard work this year that you can't, or is it just that you're scared?"

In a small whisper back, CJ said, "I dunno." With that he moved away from me and paced the side of the pool, wrapped in his towel, shivering as much from fear as cold.

Turning, he looked at me again and followed my gaze to the clock. Less than ten minutes remained before evaluations were over.

I said, "Evaluations are almost over. They said you can try again, but if you are going to do it, you need to get in the water soon. What do you think you want to do?"

CJ wrapped the towel tighter around his body and stared at the clock, then back at me. "I dunno, Mom. I just don't know," he said, with his voice in a slightly higher pitch.

I knew he was scared, but I also knew that CJ really wanted this. From his answers, it seemed he was undecided. Maybe I was wrong, but I thought the real issue was that this pool was significantly deeper than the one he had swum in last summer and winter, presenting a new challenge for CJ. If he was up to the challenge, I wanted to make sure I supported him, but I needed to see if he was up to it.

"Sweetie, I know that this pool is deeper than the one you are used to, but swimming is swimming. If you can do it there, you can do it here—no problem. Now, if you make it from one end of *this* pool to the other, you will get a prize. I know you can do it, but *you* need to choose whether you want to try. It could be today or any other day, it's up to you." Was it a bribe? Yes, but more important, I felt as if I had empowered him to choose.

I looked at CJ's face and could see the wheels turning. His face brightened as he raised it toward mine. "Like when I worked all summer at swimming and swam the full length of the other pool for the first time?" He remembered. A small wave of relief washed over me. He was willing to try.

Then—the cloud returned. "I can't do it."

Thus far he had not refused to try again, and his face had brightened when I mentioned his previous accomplishment. On some level I truly believed that he realized he was capable. At that moment I knew the issue was more about his inner belief in himself. If CJ could get past this hurdle of self-doubt, he would feel a tremendous sense of accomplishment.

Hugging CJ, I said, "You *can* do this. I know you can; you just need to believe in yourself as I believe in you."

"What happens if I have to stop because I'm scared and hold on to the side?"

"I don't care how many times you stop or hold on to the side. The most important thing is you at least try." I wished then that I could infuse my beliefs in CJ's abilities into him.

Another minute of hesitation and pacing, and then CJ dropped his towel, pulled his goggles down, and signaled to the coach that he wanted another try. Before long he was back in the water, his arms flailing, and his legs beating against the icy-cold water. He was doing it!

Walking by his side, I yelled words of encouragement: "You can do this!" or "A little more, CJ!"

With each step I watched in amazement as my son took small strokes in the pool. Every few strokes he paused to hold on to the side and to verify I was still there. My vision began to blur as tears pooled in my eyes. I couldn't believe he was doing it. Although it seemed like an eternity, he finally made it to the end and jumped out. As he looked back at the pool and then at me, a broad smile extended across his face. "I did it!"

Yes you did, CJ, yes you did.

That was not the end of the dilemma, however.

At home later that night, I recounted the day's events to Tom, my husband. I still questioned whether I had done the right thing. Yes, it had been important to motivate CJ, but I also struggled with offering prizes. Sometimes it's important to do things just because you want to challenge yourself, with the real prize coming in the form of self-satisfaction. I really did not want to start a precedent that prizes would be offered for every challenging task. However, I also realized he was still young, and rewards could be very effective if used sparingly.

Then we heard sobs coming from upstairs. We both went to CJ's room, where we found him doubled up on his bed. In halting breaths, he said, "I can't do swim team. I don't want my friends to see me fail. I want to swim again, just not with all those people around."

I looked at him, my arms wrapped around me, my right hand covering the dull pain in my heart. When he should be celebrating his accomplishment, instead he was still stressing about the pressure he might feel being on a team and having to perform in front of a crowd. Maybe he didn't immediately get in the pool and swim like he thought he would. But eventually he did get in, face his fears, and take one more step toward becoming a stronger swimmer. My son was missing the point.

I sat on the edge of his bed, pulled him into my arms, and said, "You don't have to do it, CJ. It's okay. We are proud of you for trying, even when you were scared. Today you were brave."

Today he had taken a step in believing in himself, and that in itself was a monumental accomplishment. He didn't need to be competitive to be successful but rather needed to learn that sometimes confidence comes in small amounts, each building on another.

In the end, we found a noncompetitive group for CJ to participate in. He ended his summer with a mini-meet, surrounded by his friends, their parents and us cheering him on. When CJ finished his heat and pulled himself out of the water, he simply glowed.

I believe CJ accomplished more than just swimming that summer, and I learned the importance of working with my son so he was empowered to make his own decision—even if I didn't really know what he needed.

Sometimes we lack the insight as to what our children really need. Pay attention to your child's verbal and nonverbal cues. If you think that they are capable, encourage them to try—celebrating even the smallest successes. If they choose not to move forward, or if they fail, be there to support them. Regardless, make sure the child has the space they need to make their own decision.

Daddy Isn't Coming Home

Sonja's Missing Pages: When you underestimate the impact of a situation

THE BATHROOM IN THE APARTMENT was warm and filled with the scent of Johnson & Johnson baby bath. My three-year-old son, Bobby, played amid the foamy mountains, which had the appearance of clouds against the baby-blue wall tiles. Skimming the banana-yellow duck across the water, he seemed to be enjoying himself. He submerged the duck under the water's surface. Pressure built and it reappeared, spraying water with it. Bobby's eyes intently focused on the rubber duck.

"Mommy, when's Daddy coming home?"

There it was again: the question. Each day he asked, and each day the answer was the same. This was the second time he had asked within the span of only a few hours. As I gently stroked his body with a washcloth, silence hung between us. Putting more soap on the square, worn cloth, I struggled with what to say next.

"Sweetie, Daddy is staying at the other house. Remember how Mommy and Daddy were fighting all the time? Well, we aren't going to do that anymore." Looking toward his face, searching for a connection to his big green eyes, I said, "Sweetie, look at Mommy."

Bobby stopped playing, his arm disappearing beneath the bubbles. He stared at me, his eyes locked onto mine.

The muscles in my arms and chest tensed. Spaghetti dinner rose in my throat. The ache in my heart returned. This was harder than I'd thought it would be. Taking a deep breath, I continued. It was time to do this, to really lay it out there.

"Daddy. Isn't. Coming. Home."

Bobby was silent for a moment, his blank stare unwavering. My stomach in knots, I waited for a response, any response to my words. Then he tilted his mass of brown hair back, and a primal wail swelled from him. As his cries reverberated off the bathroom walls, I stooped down and reached for him. His eyes were rolling back into his head. Pulling him out of the water, I swaddled him in a towel and gripped him tightly to me. Bobby buried his face in the terry cloth, his body shaking with each successive sob.

As he lay limp, his cries muffled by the towel, I sat there holding and rocking him back and forth, willing comfort into his small body.

A deluge of ugly, and sometimes painful, childhood memories surfaced.

Life had taught me to be a survivor. Most of my existence, and that of my six siblings, was spent traveling between foster homes or other family members' homes. When I *was* at home, my brothers and sisters and I parented each other; our mother and father often disappeared for days at a time on drinking binges. *Dysfunction* does not begin to describe my upbringing. Yet despite it all, I survived my childhood and went on to marry a decent man.

Unfortunately, Bruce and I no longer functioned well as a married couple. Despite our issues, we both loved Bobby and did our best to create a good home life for him. When the marriage began to disintegrate, I knew that I wanted to shield Bobby from the ugliness that can come from feuding spouses. By separating from Bruce, I thought I could reduce Bobby's exposure to our bickering. When I was a child, my parents did very little to shelter me from the cruelty of the world. As a parent, I was determined that I would do the exact opposite with my son. Given that I had survived with far less parental care, and that Bobby was young, I believed that this separation would be easier on him than the alternative.

My thoughts were interrupted when Bobby pulled his head away from my chest and looked up at me. His face blotted with red patches and wet with tears, his eyes pierced mine as he said fiercely, "You did this. It's your fault. You left and moved us here."

My heart began to tear, slowly, until the pain within it was unbearable—a sharp contrast to how I felt about my ending marriage.

Leaving Bruce had been a logical decision. The marriage was over, and I needed to leave. I had wanted it to be peaceful, for things to go smoothly. I thought I was doing the best thing for everyone. There wouldn't be any more angry shouting. No more tension. All had been thought through, considered, or so I'd thought. I had not counted on this. I'd expected that Bobby would be sad and we would have to work through that. I did not expect this level of anger or blame.

As I sat there on the tile floor, with my son staring accusingly into my eyes, my mind flooded. Every bit of surety washed away, baring nothing but uncertainty.

Had I truly done the right thing for us all? My childhood had taught me what not to do—refuse to make any healthy decisions and leave kids to be bounced around in the adults' muddle. But my experience was deficient in guiding me as to how to move forward. How could I do the right thing when I didn't even know what that was? Nothing in my life had been this difficult.

I carried Bobby into his room. Standing him up, I gently pulled his pajamas onto his body. Despondent, Bobby appeared suddenly smaller and frail. He no longer would look at me.

His head turned toward the wall which obscured any further observation of him, leaving me with little else to do than to tuck him into bed. I pulled the covers up around him, hoping to somehow mend his hurt. Turning toward him, my voice slightly above a whisper, I said, "Bobby, I love you." In return, I was met with . . . silence.

And not only silence, but Bobby's back was turned to me. It was a wall, shutting me out.

Perched on the edge of his bed, I was numb to everything, including my bathwater-soaked clothing, which still clung to my body. As I slowly rubbed Bobby's back, Buzz Lightyear's smirk stared back at me from his sheets. The smirk seemed to emphasize what I already knew—I had really screwed up.

We sat there silently, and over the next hour I rubbed his back trying to figure out why I had grossly underestimated how this was going to impact my son. I searched for the answer in my actions and initially couldn't arrive at anything. I thought back to my own childhood and the challenges I faced, and then for some reason I realized what might have been the missing piece: my distorted childhood had caused me to underestimate the impact this was going to have on Bobby.

Growing up, I was subject to the instability, and sometimes volatility, that arises from being a child of alcoholic parents. Along the way I learned to quiet my emotions. It was simpler to just put my head down and work through the rough points. If the issues weren't acknowledged, then in some way perhaps they weren't as bad as we thought they were. It was a way of coping, *my* way of coping. Simply put, I buried my feelings rather than expressing them, and it never dawned on me that my son might handle things differently than I would have.

Obviously I was way out of my league on this issue and I needed help. Not from self-help books or magazine articles but from an expert source. The problem? I didn't know any expert sources, and I certainly couldn't turn to my own parents. There had to be an answer.

Shortly after that night, I found myself at the library, researching parenting books and other public resources. While doing so, I came upon a group that offered counseling for divorced families. I called that day and made the commitment to go. It wasn't much, but at least it was a beginning.

Leaving my first session, I felt grounded. In the same way I'd known we had to divorce, I also knew that I was moving in the right direction. The session offered a community of other parents going through the same issues. After only one meeting, I came away with ideas and techniques I could use to ease the transition for Bobby. I may not have handled things as well as I could have, but I wasn't alone with what I was experiencing. More important, with my new knowledge, I knew that I could make things better.

Excited, I called Bruce and invited him to join me. "I support *your* need to go, Sonja. But I'm gonna pass."

Hanging up the phone, I was disappointed but not surprised. I was going to do this. Whether Bruce joined me or not, I was going to learn how to be a parent.

Through numerous sessions, I learned how to support Bobby better during the divorce process. The importance of uniformity in rules and environment, spread across both homes, became paramount. Bruce and I needed to establish and agree to similar schedules, rules, and discipline techniques.

Initially Bruce was skeptical, but with my insistence we eventually were able to agree upon a clearly defined schedule for Bobby as well as house rules and consequences. Regardless of which home Bobby was in, everything was set up similarly. The consistency made the weekly transitions easier because he didn't have to learn a new set of rules every time he moved between our houses.

With this outside help, I began to learn what it meant to be a good parent, and ironically, indirectly so did my ex.

No matter how insightful or considerate you try to be regarding your child's feelings, you may underestimate the impact of a situation. When that happens, don't be afraid to get help for yourself, your child, or even both of you.

Bullying

Sarah's Missing Pages—When your child
is suffering and you missed the clues

ADAM SAT AT THE DINNER TABLE, eyes downcast, head hung. As his younger brothers argued the merits of peas, Adam sat there pushing them with his fork from one side of the plate to the other.

"All right, guys, time to wrap it up. Dinner's over," I announced as I stood up from the table, plate in hand.

Pushing his plate away, Adam slid from his chair and quietly left the table, turning away from me.

I called to the back of his red T-shirt as he walked away. My normally vibrant six-year-old wasn't eating and wasn't responding to me. This wasn't like him, but then again there had been a few other odd things recently as well. Making a mental note to try to talk to him later, I issued my typical nighttime instructions—unsure if they were even being listened to. "Adam, I'm gonna get the boys bathed and into bed. Go brush your teeth and get into bed, and I'll tuck you in as soon as I am through."

I turned my attention back to Justin and Jonathon. Pausing, I smiled and surveyed the damage that only peas and mashed potatoes can make in an eighteen-month-old's hair. At four, Justin wasn't much better than his younger brother, preferring most days to use his shirt over a napkin. Extracting Jonathon from his high chair, I grabbed Justin's hand and brought them both into the bathroom.

As I passed Adam's room, I looked at him lying on his bed with the Lego catalog. Normally Adam studied each page, but tonight he halfheartedly flipped through it. Something was definitely off. Wrong. Tonight's bathtime for the younger boys needed to be short. It was time for Adam and me to talk.

Six weeks ago Adam began first grade. He was enthusiastic for the first four weeks. Each day he came home and would recount the day, detail by detail. Now when I asked him how it was, I received, "Some bad, some good, Mom," in return. With each progressive day, he became more and more withdrawn.

I was at a loss. Academically there didn't appear to be any issues, and he had never had any problems socially. A gentle boy, Adam had sandy blond hair, green eyes, and a smile made crooked by his recent loss of a front tooth. Eager to please, he never had a problem making friends and seemed to get along with everyone.

"Good night, boys," I said as I partially closed the door to the younger boys' room. I walked the few steps to Adam's door. Standing there with my hand on the knob, I took a deep breath before walking in.

Sitting on the edge of his bed, I nudged his shoulder until he finally looked at me. Adam obviously did not want to meet my gaze; instead, he lay there focusing on the edge of his blanket.

"Adam, what's going on? You don't seem that happy any-more when you come home from school."

"It's nothin', Mom," he replied as he turned his head away to study the print on his wall.

"It *is* something, Adam. You don't seem to like school any-more. What's going on? Is it your teacher? Is it someone in your class?" Tears rolled down his cheeks. "Adam, please, you can tell me anything."

"There's a boy at school. He doesn't like me, and I don't know why."

My dread turned to momentary relief. *It's just a friend issue.* Although tough, this kind of thing is merely a part of growing up.

Reaching out, I gently touched his arm. "Oh, honey, that happens. You can't get along with everyone. And sometimes people just don't want to be your friend."

"No, Mommy." Adam rolled over, his face a mixture of intensity and fear.

"He doesn't like me. He keeps telling me that his mom is a cop who has knives and guns. And that he's gonna shoot me and cut me. I'm scared, Mommy. Why would he want to hurt me?"

The blood drained from my face. Guns, knives, threats?

I sat there paralyzed, unable to produce a single consoling word. Who tells any child they are going to shoot them and cut them up? What kind of world was this other little boy living in? We don't live in an urban area—not that it would be acceptable there either—but I could almost understand it if we did. This simply doesn't happen in the small town that we live in. Why did this boy think it was okay to say these things?

Then my momentary shock was gone. The muscles in my jaw, arms, and back tensed up as the anger flowed through me. Pausing, I took a deep breath.

"We'll get through this, sweetie," I said, stroking Adam's forehead. "The other little boy is just angry, Adam. I guess he's taking his anger out on you. It isn't right and I don't know why he's doing it, but we're gonna solve this problem." Bending down, I kissed his forehead, as I had every night since he was born. As I got up and crossed the room, I glanced at the fire trucks that adorned his walls. The innocence of these images was at odds with the harshness of the story my son had just shared with me.

Part of me was incredulous that this was happening now, when he was this young. When I was growing up, there were bullies, but I remember them more in junior high and high school. In the past few years, issues of bullying had made the news, but again most of them were focused on children of middle school age or older. I had categorized bullying as something that might happen in the future, not something my child would face in elementary school—much less first grade.

Leaving Adam's room, I walked directly to the computer. Although there was no way to reach the school that night, I knew I had to do something. Shaking, I composed an e-mail to the teacher, principal, and guidance counselor. In it I outlined everything from Adam, including the other child's name, when the first instance happened, and how it had progressed over the last two weeks. Going on, I detailed how Adam's behavior had changed and how it was getting progressively worse. As I clicked Send, a small weight was lifted, but I did not feel altogether relieved. I was haunted by the fact that I probably should have done more, or at least known this was going on before tonight.

Standing at the sink, I stared blankly out the window. Instead of the outside, all I saw were images of the playground bullying. The face of the other child flashed before me and I turned away. I knew that face. I had seen him every week when I volunteered in the classroom.

I should have seen something, some indication of what was happening. Despite having my hands full with the two younger boys, I had noticed some behavior changes in Adam. I thought perhaps it was possibly the transition between kindergarten and the more structured first grade curriculum. The roughness of this transition was something that the other moms in my moms' group had warned me about.

I wasn't an absent parent; I was very involved and active in the classroom. Regardless, somehow I had missed this and my son had been scared for weeks. For weeks he had sat threatened, and I had been unaware, unable to see it or help him avoid it.

With the kids safely in bed, I went to our room and called my husband, who was away on an extended business assignment. We discussed what Adam had shared and what I had already done to begin addressing it. Until I was able to speak to someone about it and hear how they were going to handle it, there wasn't much more to be done. Unfortunately this, like most parenting matters, fell solely to me when my husband was away like this.

Hanging up the phone, I wondered how I was going to fall asleep. Eventually the sound of the late September crickets put me into a restless slumber.

Daylight streamed into my room, waking me up well before the alarm clock. Wrapping a bathrobe around me, I went into the kitchen and began my morning ritual. Grateful for the quiet reprieve, I sat there contemplating how to handle the day. Positive and reassuring: that was what I needed to be. I took another deep breath, closed my eyes, and tried to picture myself smiling and confident. Instead, my shoulders slumped and a tear came down my face.

Before the coffeemaker finished brewing, I poured myself a large mug. Sitting there dazed, I sipped the coffee, listening as the hot water dripped through the grounds, refilling the coffee-pot. Thoughts of Adam's classroom filled my head. I wasn't sure how I was going to send him to school that day. I was torn between having him attend class to maintain normalcy and keeping him home—which might enhance his fear.

Sending Adam off, I hugged and kissed him and told him that we were going to work it all out. Adam looked back at me from the window of the yellow school bus as it pulled away, and I hoped that I was right and that it would be resolved—*immediately*.

After he left, I followed up with the school on the phone. In speaking with the principal and guidance counselor, they assured me that it would be handled quickly; with knots in my stomach, I hoped that the school was being truthful. I was surprised and relieved by the expediency of their response.

By one o'clock that afternoon, I received an e-mail back from the principal. In the small span of the morning, the school had contacted the other child's parents, met with them, and begun counseling both boys. Given the increased awareness and occurrences of bullying, the school had enacted an extremely swift protocol to address the issue—critical when working with a child as young as six.

The healing process continued throughout the year, and Adam has recovered well. Although the conflict for him resolved, it took me longer to let myself off the hook. The experience left me initially feeling hypervigilant. I had missed things in the past and wanted to make sure that I didn't miss things again. Then, even though Adam appeared to be doing okay, I continued to make it a point to engage him about school, and I checked in regularly with his teachers and administration. I have come to realize that even the most "involved" parent can still miss things.

We are human, and even if you communicate well with your child and are very "involved" with his life, you will miss things. Give yourself permission to be human, and trust that you will act when necessary.

H-E-Double-Hockey-Sticks

Shaney's Missing Pages: When your child has questions about beliefs that you can't answer

"MOM, I MISS CASSY."

I looked toward the corner of the kitchen where Cassy, our dog who was with us for twelve years, used to sleep. The area was near three large windows, which offered her hours of sunbeams within which to nap.

"I know, honey. But she's up in heaven running around chasing a ball or something." I smiled at the thought of her; I too missed our dog and wished she hadn't died last month.

"Well, that's where I wanna go," Jake said, between popping grapes in his mouth.

In the midst of loading the dishwasher, I said, "Mm-hm."

"Mom, I *really* don't want to go to the hockey stick place."

"What?"

Jake's blue eyes stared intently at me. "You know, the hockey place. *The 'H-E-double-hockey-sticks' place.*"

Standing up, I threw my head back and let out an enormous laugh.

This is why I love my children. At some point he had picked up my code word for *hell*—H-E-double-hockey-sticks. I could only imagine what he was picturing. Someplace really hot with a bunch of hockey sticks floating around?

I went over to the well-worn kitchen table where he was seated, hugged him, and gave him a little kiss on his head. Cassy's recent passing was obviously at the root of this discussion and Jake's concerns, or so I thought. "Sweetie, I don't think you'll have anything to worry about."

The dryer buzzed, and I walked across the cool kitchen tile to the laundry room. As I folded the clothes, I heard Jake's little voice singing in the kitchen. It was a song he had learned at the Jewish Community Center, where he attended preschool. Jake and his younger sister, Drew, had been going to the JCC for several years. The JCC had a great preschool program, and although there were children of all faiths there, we figured they might also have a bit more exposure to their Jewish faith as well.

I pulled up the fully loaded laundry basket and turned to walk back into the kitchen. Just as I did, the singing stopped.

"Mom, why am I Jewish?"

Bewildered, I wondered how we got from missing our dog to heaven and hell to Jake questioning why he was Jewish. I stood there in the middle of the kitchen, my laundry basket suspended in midair.

This was not going to be as simple as I thought.

Jake and his sister were being raised as Reform Jews, like their father. I was, well, nothing really. I was raised with no real religious background. The first time I ever set foot in a church was in college, and even then it was at the request of my boyfriend at the time. Sure, my family celebrated Christian holidays, but they were more out of a social norm than true religious significance.

"Jake, let me put the laundry in my room. When I get back, we can talk about this." It was a stall tactic, but I needed a few moments to gather myself and think about what I was going to say.

Before Steve and I got married, we discussed having children and how we wanted to raise them. We decided our children would learn Jewish history and traditions, but there wouldn't be the strict observance of all the Jewish laws. This gave us the flexibility to incorporate some of the Christian holidays, which were celebrated in my family. We blended a few and celebrated what we call "Christmakah." We have a menorah and light it, next to the Christmas tree, during the winter holidays. Up until now, we hadn't had any in-depth questions from the kids regarding our faith or beliefs.

I walked back into the kitchen and sat down next to Jake. Unfortunately, the stalling could not compensate for the fact that I had no defined religion and had not personally explored my religious beliefs—not even to the base level my six-year-old son was doing right now. Hoping an additional question might trigger some kind of brilliant parental response, where I might be able to adequately answer his question, I probed him.

"Why do you ask?"

"Because most of the other kids at the JCC and around here are Catholic or something. Nobody here really is Jewish."

He was right. There weren't a lot of people around us who were Jewish. None of our neighbors were, and most of his friends from the preschool at the Jewish Community Center weren't Jewish. Obviously some of the children there were Jewish, but Jake wasn't really close to any of them.

"Jake, you and Drew are being raised as Reform Jews, just like Daddy and Grandpa. We want you to understand the history of the Jewish people because this is part of who you are. But it isn't everything. A lot of people can get caught up in labeling people. Yes, you're Jewish, but you're also so much more than that."

"Okay. I guess I get it, Mom," Jake said as he got up from the table to play in his room.

Watching him walk away, I honestly wasn't certain if he got it—or if I did either. Luckily Jake seemed to be content with my response—for now. But I knew that this would not be the end of the questions; I also knew that the broad generalizations that Steve and I had agreed on were not going to be enough. Right now, it was about understanding the basic differences of organized religions. Jake was beginning to seek structure, similar to those in other areas of his life, but soon enough he would seek details that we had not defined adequately enough. He was starting to try to understand what it meant to be a certain faith and was looking for direction from his parents. How could I direct him well when I myself was not clear?

I realized that although I didn't have a formal religious upbringing and couldn't provide Jake with all the details, my broad perspective might also be an advantage. Through my own lack of organized religion, I developed a profound respect for a variety of religious and spiritual beliefs. While I wanted my children to grow and develop within the Jewish religion, I also wanted them to understand that religion and spirituality can come in many forms, and none is necessarily right or better than the other. At the end of each day, I wanted my children to be able to look in the mirror and know that they had been a good person, friend, brother or sister, son or daughter, *regardless* of what religion they were.

That brief experience raised to the forefront that Steve and I had more work to do in defining what we wanted for our children religiously. Ultimately the key for us will be to find a balance that suits both our parental goals and an understanding that where that balance is may change over time.

What also became apparent was that it was time for me to dig a little deeper into my own religious and spiritual beliefs so when this comes up again, and it will, I may just be a bit better prepared.

Sometimes the missing page is our own belief system. We teach our children our beliefs on many things: appropriate food, ethics, morals, and so on, but religion is complicated. If you haven't taken the time, take a moment and really think about what you believe; it will help you clarify the message that you are sending your child. Be prepared to give your child the space they need to discover their own spirituality and the understanding that it may be different than yours.

New Parent Crisis

*Diane's Missing Pages: When you are intelligent,
competent, and just in over your head*

STANDING IN THE KITCHEN, I put Kevin into his portable infant car seat and strapped him in. Although we weren't going anywhere, I wanted him in a safe place while I gathered myself. Immediately, he went into wild man mode. I looked down to his tiny body and watched as he screamed—and I mean *screamed*. For a few moments I merely sat there looking at him, wondering what I had done wrong, why he couldn't settle down, and why he would not sleep.

Ever.

They always tell you, "Nap when the baby naps." Whoever advised this never met my son. Each day he would wake at five a.m. and would eventually settle down by eight p.m. Then he would be awake off and on through the night to feed until the whole process started over. My entire existence was spent trying to get him to be content and nap.

I adjusted the handle of the carrier-style seat down, propping the seat up on the kitchen floor so that I could see Kevin. I slid the sliding glass door open, stepped outside onto the patio stairs, and closed it behind me. Perched on the patio stairs I looked at him from the other side of the glass. Visions of me pulling away from the house in my car or just walking away through the woods behind my home filled my head. I was searching for anything to escape this place and responsibility.

Instead, I sat on the steps. I could still hear him, but his screaming was muffled now.

Wrapping my arms around myself, I turned from him and dropped my head to my chest in dismay. What had happened to me? All my life I was driven, had it together, and knew what I wanted. I had a college degree, doctoral degree, and postgraduate residency. I had waited to get married, and at thirty-five I married the man of my dreams. We were both excited to start a family and were thrilled with Kevin's arrival. I had always excelled at everything and somehow thought being a parent would be easier than this.

Tears spilled down my face, dotting my red shirt with crimson spots.

Looking in at my baby boy, I wondered how it was that this tiny seven-pound infant could reduce me to this. In the glass looking back at me was a woman with rumpled clothes, unkempt hair, and dark circles under her eyes, which were now red and swollen from crying. The self-assured doctor that I once had been was missing.

The tears turned into a sob, and before long, the only crying I heard was my own. I didn't hear my husband, Todd, arrive.

"Diane, what's going on?"

I turned my head toward him but couldn't muster an

answer. I wondered what must be going through his head as he looked past me to our son on the other side of the glass door.

"I don't know."

As I continued to sob, Todd held me.

"I don't know if I can do this. Nothing I do is right. You'd think I would have the smarts to know how to care for and quiet my son. I don't what he needs! I don't know how to be a good mom! Why did I think I could do this?"

Todd gently smoothed my hair and wiped my tears.

"D, you can do this. There are many women who do it every day. I think we need to start with what *you* need."

After coming home from the hospital I had tried to be what I thought a mom should be. Up until now when life added responsibilities, I took them in stride. I had always been able to manage the challenges presented to me and still maintain some sense of normalcy.

The life I was living now felt anything but normal. My child never slept and at times endlessly cried. Because of that I rarely slept or bathed or cleaned the house or did the laundry or anything. Not only did I feel like I wasn't being a good mother, there were days where all I did was awaken and wander through the day like a zombie, unable even to manage the basic things I had done before Kevin was born. I was beaten down and exhausted. I couldn't do this alone anymore.

In that moment I stopped crying, took a deep breath, and realized exactly what I needed.

"I need help, Todd." Admitting this and letting go of the notion that I could be that "supermom" humbled me.

For the next few minutes we talked through a plan.

The most important thing we realized, practically speaking, was that I needed more sleep. Despite Todd's long commute, he agreed he would get up now in the middle of the night and handle the late-night feedings until I regained some sanity through some much-needed rest. The tailspin that had been my existence felt like it was coming to a stop. Actively working with Todd through the plan, in which he assumed additional parenting responsibilities, reduced my feelings of isolation. I realized that even an intelligent, competent person can still find herself in over her head where she needs help.

In the days that followed, we devised alternative solutions to help Kevin sleep in the middle of the day. We asked family and friends for ideas and researched on the Internet. Ultimately, with blackout shades for his room, a white noise machine, and a strict napping schedule, he came around.

As he did, I made sure that I napped too—for however short a time period that it was.

And—supermom no more—I accepted the fact that the piles of laundry and dishes were just going to have to wait.

Holding yourself to a "super parent" standard will only isolate you. Don't be afraid to ask for help. No matter who you are, the only school offering a degree in parenting is the school of hard knocks.

Children Develop
on Their Timeline

*Danielle's Missing Pages: When you compare
your children—unjustly*

STEPPING INTO THE GARAGE, David stood next to his royal-blue Husky bike. Dutifully putting his helmet on, he glanced back at Grace and me. At four he had well outgrown the double stroller, which meant that Grace would just have to go it alone in the stroller today.

Looking at him, I wondered if he had grown overnight. David was tall and lanky like Keagan, his older brother. His bleached blond hair peaked out from underneath his helmet. David's green eyes peered back at me, as if to direct me that it was time to go.

The morning was hot and humid, not uncommon for June. As usual, we began our morning run with David pedaling ahead and me doing a walk/run combination behind him. It was a constant start and stop as we made it through our neighborhood streets.

"Hey Ma, there's a frog over there in that pond! Do ya see it?"

David had come to a complete standstill, admiring the beauty of a frog on the edge of our neighbor's pond. As I pushed his rear bicycle wheel with the front wheel of the jogging stroller, my reply was simply, "Yeah, it's great, honey. Let's keep moving."

Between periodic nudges along our morning route, I found myself studying David. He looked much like Keagan and Grace but was utterly different. Keagan, at age seven, was the consummate jock, academic, and charmer; Grace, at two, was just as charming and sociable. David, however, at four, was none of these things. David was the clumsy kid who was happy simply playing in the mulch at the playground while other kids played around him.

Keagan learned to ride the bike right before turning three; David, when he was almost four. Everything came easy for Keagan; David struggled, and he was reaching milestones later than his brother. Keagan was into basketball, baseball, and soccer, while David was bored with most activities and would prefer to sit and play video games instead.

As a parent I knew I shouldn't compare them, but still it was there. My husband and I got along easily with Keagan and understood him. He was our first child and we had learned what worked for him. When David was born, we cared for him as we had Keagan. Because he was my second boy, I figured his interests would be similar to Keagan's as well. To avoid future perceptions of inequality between the brothers, we made sure that David had all the same opportunities that Keagan had had. Unfortunately, I think this unintentionally laid the groundwork for the inevitable comparison of the two boys.

We ran David through the same courses of athletics that

Keagan had done at a similar age. In each instance, he would tire of it in minutes and want to be taken home. Over and over again we found ourselves saying, "Just ten more minutes, honey!" Everything was ten minutes. Thank goodness he couldn't tell time yet.

We could see he wasn't into the sports. When David went out onto the field he would look at me, his eyes asking permission to quit, and yet we pushed him back onto the field in our over-zealous attempt to ensure equality between him and his brother. More important, I don't think we understood what really *did* interest him.

David had stopped again. The sun pounded down on me; a drip of sweat hung off the tip of my nose.

"Ma, did you ever wonder about grasshoppers?"

"No, I haven't, really. What about them?"

"Why do you think they can hop so far?" David responded, intently examining a grasshopper sitting on a bright blade of grass.

"Well, maybe we can look it up on the Web when we get home, okay? Now let's keep moving, before it gets too hot!" I nudged his wheel again, and he started to pedal once more.

We were about two miles into our three-mile circuit that morning, and I wished there were some way to shorten it. Although the heat was beginning to get to me, I frankly was tired of constantly having to nudge David along. When David was younger and in the carriage with Keagan riding in front on a bike, Keagan would often ride ahead of me and go in circles until I caught up. I never had to push him along, Keagan would just ride. Why couldn't David ride along like his older brother had?

David had paused again. Just as I was about to nudge him again, he exclaimed, "Mom! Look there's a heron. It's so cool!"

Not able to move forward without David moving too, I stopped. I saw him looking at me, wanting me to really *see* what he saw.

Then the bird gracefully ascended into the air, its reflection mirrored on the canal below. I saw, perhaps for the first time, my son really enrapt with something. I studied his face as he studied the movement of the bird.

David turned his head toward me and our eyes met. I had connected with David and shared in something that really engaged him, something that had nothing to do with his brother.

All of a sudden he took off.

"David! Stop. Stop. Slow down!" By now I was yelling at him. He stopped just ahead of the stop sign and looked back at me. He had done a complete reversal. David was no longer poking along but racing in front. A smile spread across his face, and then he began to ride in circles.

The water gathered in my eyes as I realized then how unrealistic my expectations had been. He wasn't Keagan and wasn't going to get excited by or excel at the same things his older brother did—a point that I had overlooked until this morning. As the tears intermingled with the sweat, I smiled back at him.

"Come on, Ma, move faster. Let's get home before it gets too hot!" And with that David took off. I watched him during the final straightaway toward our house and couldn't keep up. At that moment, I didn't care. I felt as if something had profoundly changed that morning.

In the ensuing months I watched as David began to get more interested in different things. Ironically one of them was baseball, a sport we had previously introduced him to. The difference was he was now doing it for himself, not us, and was having a blast.

During that otherwise normal run when I watched the heron take flight, and watched David take off, it crystallized for me that regardless of similarities, my children all need the freedom to be different and develop their own interests, on their own timetables and in their own way.

Parenting is continual problem solving. It is human nature to learn from your experience and apply these lessons and expectations to the next. Unfortunately that doesn't always work with parenting. The reality is that what works for one child may not work for the other. Help your children by giving each the opportunity to grow, explore, and discover at their pace.

Winging It

Mike's Missing Pages: When you hope you have every detail covered

DELIA AND I WERE EXTREMELY EXCITED when we found out that she was pregnant. We wanted to be sure—really sure—that we were ready for when our child was born. In spite of the fact that she had worked in a hospital caring for babies, and we both had helped out with our nieces and nephews, we still researched and prepared for our baby. We read everything possible, from parenting books to consumer reports, on anything infant related. If there was a safety gadget or, hey, any baby gadget, we had it— including a wipe warmer.

Delia gave birth after two days of labor. It had not been easy and did not go at all according to our birthing plan, but the moment she delivered our baby girl, I was amazed. Here was this new little person. The nurses quickly whisked the baby away and cleaned her up. We received her back swaddled neatly in a blanket, a pink knit cap on her head.

Before we brought our daughter, Lauren, home, I went to our Baltimore row house and performed a pre-baby-arrival inspection. My wife was very organized and there wasn't much to inspect, but I wanted to make sure just in case.

As we were getting ready to leave the hospital, the nurses went through our discharge instructions, handed us a complimentary diaper bag filled with samples and pamphlets, and asked if we had any questions. We really didn't have any at the time and were anxious to get out of the hospital and begin our new life with our daughter.

The trip home went off without incident. I remember walking through the door feeling confident that everything was in order and Delia would be pleased. Lauren's outfits were organized and tucked away in her dresser. The wipes were warm and all the items we would need to change her and tend to her belly button were close at hand. We made it through the first round of breast-feedings without issue. Delia finished logging the baby's most recent feeding and wet diaper into our baby journal, then turned to me and said, "Mike, we need to bathe her."

"What? Today?"

"Yeah, I think so. She hasn't had a bath since she was born. I think she is supposed to be bathed today."

"Well, if my baby girl is gonna need a bath, then we're gonna bathe her." I smiled. How hard could this be? "What do we need to do?"

At this point, Delia was burping our little Lauren. She looked at me with a blank gaze. "Uh, I don't know. I mean, Mike, I *really* don't know." I saw the panic rising in her.

"Don't we have a bathtub and a bunch of washing stuff? I'll go get it." I could do this, I thought. Bathing a baby shouldn't be terribly difficult.

I walked back into the room carrying the baby tub, soap, washcloths, towels, some water temperature gadget, diapers, clothes, wipes, and ointment—everything I thought we would need.

"Here we go. I've got all the washing things. Let's get this tubby going for our baby girl."

Delia looked up from where she was sitting and asked, "But where should we bathe her?"

Standing in our living room, looking at my wife, I tried not to be a smartass and say, "In the tub, where else?" Although the thought crossed my mind, I held my tongue.

As if she sensed my impending sarcastic remark, she continued, "I *mean*, do you think we should bathe her in the kitchen or bathroom? The kitchen is sunny and warm, and we can stand up. Or do you think that the bathroom would be better?"

How the hell was I supposed to know? Both have water. Why should it matter?

I surveyed the options and said, "I'm thinking the bathroom. You stay here; I'll get everything ready, okay? No worries."

Making my way up the stairs, I heard Delia add, "But she needs to be warm. I think we need to bring in a little heater." I couldn't believe that I heard her right. A heater? Really? Not wanting to upset my wife, I pulled out the little space heater from my office.

I walked into the bathroom with this odd-shaped infant tub full of baby gear and set up the heater, cautious about keeping it away from the water. Surrounded by cheerful duck décor, I looked around and realized I didn't know where to put the baby tub. Although it would make sense to place it inside the real tub, I could also put it up by the sink or on the floor.

Since I had to get water into the baby tub, I settled on putting it into the real tub. Methodically, I took all of the plentiful baby paraphernalia out of it and placed everything carefully on a towel that I'd spread out on the floor near the real tub.

I started the water and tested it first with my hand. Not too cold, not too hot. I remembered this from when we took care of our nephew when he was about six months old. On the towel lay the infant water tester that doubled as a toy duck. On the bottom, the duck had a scale—blue for too cold, green for the correct temperature (90–100 degrees Fahrenheit), and red for too hot. Putting the duck in the water, I tested it—we were green and good to go.

As Delia walked in with Lauren, she looked at the baby tub, which at this point was overflowing with water, the duck floating on top.

"Mike, I think that's too much water."

"Well, how much water do we need?"

"It's a sponge bath, so I don't know . . . however much you need for that," Delia replied.

"Don't you have some instructions or something in one of your books on how to do this?" I hated to ask the obvious, but we had an entire library of baby-related references. My memory was blank. I didn't remember reading about the first bath, or the nurses even discussing it. There had to be something in one of our books.

"Go down into the baby bag we brought home from the hospital. They have a guide on caring for your newborn." Delia replied, her tone revealing her exasperation.

"Right! Okay, sure, let me grab it."

Returning with a folded paper that reminded me more of a map than a book, I opened it up and spread it on the bathroom floor. Delia sat on the toilet holding the baby. You would think that it was written in another language. I read it, reread it, and still didn't understand what exactly they wanted me to do. The illustrations were less than helpful. At minimum, it was obvious that I had to pour out most of the water in the tub, which I did. Now it was on to the next step.

Delia looked tired, and her patience was thinning. "Well? What do we do?"

I consulted the "baby map."

"Okay, it says start with the eyes."

Delia looked at me expectantly. "Where on the eyes?"

"Uh, go from the corner of the eyes from the area closest to the nose and pull your washcloth gently out to the hairline."

I watched as my wife navigated the small washcloth over the tiny face of our newborn.

"Now what?" she asked.

Fumbling with the baby map, I looked for the next series of directions. It gave detailed instructions on washing the baby's hair, but cautioned against getting the child too wet or she might get chilled. What? Just how are we supposed to do that, I wondered? It is a bath, after all; you have to get the baby wet. How do you avoid from getting her too wet and possibly chilled? I must have had a blank look on my face, because the next thing I knew, Delia had handed me our daughter and grabbed the baby map.

With the baby map between us, I awkwardly held my little girl. She was so small. I was almost afraid to move because I didn't want to jostle her. Instead I cautiously held her out, slightly away from my body for fear I might move the wrong way and smother her or something.

The map descended, and Delia's shoulders sagged.

"Well?" I said in a half-mocking tone, smiling at her.

"I have cared for babies in the NICU. I have my master's. You have a college degree. And we have no freaking idea how to bathe our daughter! How is that, Mike? How is it that we are this clueless?" Delia's concerned transitioned into a smile . . . and before I knew it, we were both laughing. I think we both saw humor in the fact that despite all of our preparations, we still didn't know how to complete what was a really basic task. But it had to get done, even if it wasn't 100 percent right.

Looking at Lauren's precious little body, I said, "Well, baby girl, I guess we're just gonna wing this tubby."

Despite our best intentions, sometimes
parenting is about "winging it."
Trust your instincts and it will all work out.

"You're . . . Pregnant?"

Tracy's Missing Pages: When a child's decision changes their life and everyone else's, too

THE APRIL SKY WAS FILLED with a pinkish afterglow from the sunset. The air was warm, but the coolness of the evening began to chill my skin. The back porch has always been my personal retreat, a sanctuary from the craziness of mothering my three biological children and the niece whose custody I assumed seven years ago.

My oldest son, Ben, was eighteen years old and getting ready to graduate from high school. My other two biological children, Lacey and Joseph, were fourteen and thirteen, respectively. All three of my biological children were compliant, easygoing kids. Lacey was more social than the boys, but other than that they were all very similar. However at fifteen, Jill was a bit of a wild child and aside from being strong academically, she contrasted greatly with the others.

Jill's mother was an alcoholic and drug user. She was deemed unfit as a parent when Jill was eight. Unlike my other children, Jill was always was looking for ways to push the envelope with rules, clothing choices—pretty much everything. She was a free spirit who dressed differently and didn't care what other people thought of her. Unfortunately this also felt like it translated to us too—whenever we were trying to parent her. Over the years I had tried my best with her, but she was different and far more rebellious than my other children.

Staring out into the yard, I was making mental notes of all that needed to be done to prepare for spring. My solitude was broken by the sound of the screen door opening.

"Aunt Tracy? Can I talk to you?"

My internal alarm sounded. Jill never asked to speak to me. Although I was her guardian, she usually confided in my husband, Tony, who had been the only father figure she had ever known. I couldn't imagine what this was about.

"Sure, honey, sit down."

Jill slumped into a chair opposite me, her eyes downcast. I don't know how much time went by, probably only a few minutes, but it felt longer. Jill sat there in complete silence. The longer she sat, the more frantically she picked at the hem around the sleeve of her pink hooded sweatshirt and the more concerned I became.

"Jill?"

She looked up at me. Her eyes betrayed her anxiety. And then it came spilling out.

"I'm pregnant."

"What? How?" I blurted. "You were supposed to be on the pill, for heaven's sake! Have you not been taking it?"

"I mean, it's all gonna be all right, Aunt Tracy. Theo and I are gonna keep it, and it's gonna be all right."

"You clearly have no idea what you're talking about! It's not gonna be *all right*. Your whole life is about to change. *Everything* will be different," I shouted.

Jill stood up, crossed her arms, and looked at me, her mouth drawn in a thin line. "Well, I think it's gonna be just fine," she said. With that she stomped away, slamming the back door—the door she *never* remembers to shut.

I grabbed my pack of cigarettes from the table, and my hands shook as I lit one. My stomach turned in anxious knots as if it were me who was pregnant again. Inhaling, my eyes closed, I saw myself at nineteen. I pulled my sweater tighter around my body, as if this would somehow contain the emotions raging inside me. Barely out of high school and pregnant for the first time, I'd had no idea how I was going to raise a child at nineteen. I remember feeling ill-equipped to even be an adult at that time, much less a mother. The fact that Jill seemed so naively confident baffled me. Perhaps it was because she was only fifteen.

Remembering that fact shook me that much more.

Putting my cigarette out, I stood up, took a deep breath, and walked inside to find Tony. As I passed my other children in the family room, I avoided their gaze. They knew something was wrong, but I was not prepared to discuss it.

I could hear Tony working on something in the basement. I called down to him from the top of the stairs. "Tony, can you meet me on the back porch?"

He looked up at me, a rag dangling from his hands. "Sure. I'll be right there," he replied. After our being together for nineteen years, he was able to pick up the note of urgency in my voice.

I returned to the back porch, sat at the table, and tried to compose myself. Still in shock myself, I had a difficult time calming my racing heart, but I knew it would be even harder on Tony if I was a wreck.

Opening the back door, he stepped hesitantly out onto the porch, unsure of what he was about to hear.

"Okay, Tracy, what is it?"

I lit another cigarette and exhaled. "Jill is pregnant."

"What?" he shouted. "What the hell happened? I thought we got her on the pill earlier than we wanted so this *wouldn't* happen! She's a kid, even younger than we were."

Tony clenched his jaw and looked away from me. Tension and anger filled the air. We sat that way for several minutes. Not speaking, both of us remained there trying somehow to make sense of it all. Finally I broke the silence. "She plans on keeping it."

Cocking his head sideways, Tony looked at me and said, "How's she going to do that? How is she going to pay for it? Where are they going to live? Jill and Lacey share a room; it isn't fair for Lacey to have to share with Jill and a baby. Hell, having them on that floor with all of the other kids is going to be completely disruptive to everyone."

Slamming the rag onto the table in frustration, Tony looked away from me again.

Even younger than we were. Maybe those words had gotten through to me, gotten through my anger and fear, to simple reality. I was going to be a young grandmother, just as my mother had been.

When I'd told my own parents, they were supportive—but with limits. Both of my parents were glad we'd decided to keep the baby, but they also made it clear that it was our baby to take care of. Their unconditional support and love of me was something I knew I wanted to replicate for Jill. However, that was where the comparisons ended, in part driven by the fact that I was legally an adult when I got pregnant. Jill was a minor and we were raising other, younger children, a factor that complicated things significantly for us. Whatever we worked through, we needed to take all of these things into consideration.

"Regardless of how disruptive a baby is going to be," I said, "we need to come up with something. I'm glad she came to us and glad that she is keeping it; those things we need to support. Nothing is going to change what has happened. At this point, all we can control is how we communicate this to the other children . . . and then do our best to see that her decision does not negatively impact their lives too much."

In that moment my anger gave way to an overwhelming sadness. Jill's whole life was about to change completely, and I had no way to protect her from it. There wouldn't be any more carefree Friday nights. No more hanging out with her friends, where all she would worry about was what was going on at school, the latest dating drama, and cheering at football games. That would all disappear.

Over the next hour, Tony and I discussed our options. Jill's decision to keep the baby could not be to the detriment of the rest of the family. The remaining children had not made this choice and should not have their lives completely turned upside down. Doing so would only provide the basis for future resentment. Ultimately Tony and I worked out a detailed plan for how we could support Jill but still balance the needs of the rest of the family.

We called Jill back out to the porch. Tony and I sat at the table next to each other holding hands. This wasn't going to be easy, but we would get through it, just as we had a great number of things.

When Jill came out, she stood there with her head downcast, her fists firmly planted in the pockets of her sweatshirt.

"Honey, sit down," I said, motioning to the chair across from us.

Jill looked up slightly, nudged the chair out, and slumped into it.

"First, we love you and support the fact that you want to keep the baby," I said.

Jill surveyed us warily but said nothing.

Tony looked at her. His ice-blue eyes betrayed the anger and sadness that lurked behind them. Clearing his throat, he said, "But we want you to know that this is your life, your child, and your responsibility. Frankly, Jill, I'm really disappointed. We've talked about this over and over again. You knew what your Aunt Tracy and I went through, and if there was one thing . . ."

He stopped midsentence and looked away. Seeing this, Jill averted her eyes from mine and studied the edge of the table.

I knew how much this was killing him. This was one lesson, the one warning we had tried to impart to our children: *Don't have your children young.* Yet it had happened. We wanted our children to have and enjoy their teenage and college years, without the burden of having to care for a child. His anger, like mine, was not at the situation but that we had been unable to prevent this. We had tried to give Jill a better life. I'd thought that I could be a better mother to her; instead I felt that I was a failure.

Picking up where he left off, I said, "We'll finish the basement off, so you'll have a larger area to live with the baby. This will give you the privacy you need to feed it in the middle of the night and give you both room, and give us the ability to keep things as normal as possible for the rest of the family. Theo will be able to come over and care for the baby during the daytime and early evening, but beyond that, it'll be your responsibility. If there are serious issues, we'll be here to help."

Jill looked at us expectantly, wondering what was next.

Tony and I exchanged glances, and I continued. "Jill, while we support your decision to keep the child, it is important for you to know that this decision impacts not just you and Theo, but all of us. Yes, this baby will be your responsibility, but we'll inevitably have to assume additional responsibility as well. Our lives, and that of the other kids, will change. "

The blank stare I received in return made me wonder if anything I was saying was getting through to her. I'm sure she thought this was just about her and Theo, but the reality was far greater than that. There would be doctor's visits that she would need to be driven to. There would be times where the baby would be crying in the middle of the night, making it difficult for the rest of the family to sleep. It was going to be a lot of work on Jill's part and, although I didn't mind her asking for help, I didn't want her to push off her responsibilities on others—which I had seen her do in the past with her weekly chores. It was going to be costly too, and we knew she wouldn't be able to absorb all of this, which meant we would also have to chip in and that money would be at the expense of something else.

I closed with, "Ben, Lacey, and Joseph deserve to have their lives continue as normally as possible. Part of what you need to do is respect that and not try to get them to assume what should be your responsibilities with this baby. Do you understand?"

"Thank you," Jill replied quietly. "I told you that it was gonna be all right, Aunt Tracy." With that, she hopped up and walked back into the house.

Deflated, I wondered if it was going to be all right, since it was clear that Jill appeared to not have absorbed anything my husband and I had said.

Later that evening, we held a family meeting and allowed Jill to share her news and how we were going to move forward as a family. And over the next several months, we worked to finish the living space and made all the arrangements and preparations for accepting this new child into our home. The children, including Jill, continued on as normally as possible. Despite our attempts to educate her and prepare her for what to come, she seemed to minimize the impact that the birth of the child would have.

Within three days of arriving home from the hospital, Jill announced that she wanted her boyfriend to stay the night to help with the feedings. Maybe it was the reality of the work involved, I don't know, but we would not allow it. They might have gotten pregnant, but we were not going to allow them to play house.

When we wouldn't allow it, she and the baby moved in with Theo's family. We didn't like her decision and were upset that despite being supportive—going out of our way to create space for her and the baby—she walked out. I think ultimately it boiled down to Jill realizing that this was way more than she expected. While we couldn't, and wouldn't, assume the role of parent to her new child, Theo's family would. They didn't have any other children and therefore had the capacity, and were willing, to care for the baby while Jill finished high school early and resumed a lot of her old life. At that point it became what was best for the baby, and in working with Theo's parents, we felt it was the best alternative.

As parents we have to accept that despite our best efforts, our children will make choices that we cannot control. Even in supporting them, we can be challenged. Do your best to explain to your child the full impact that her choices will have on not just her but everyone involved so that she is not surprised by the resulting fallout.

Jeans in the Freezer and Vodka in Hand

Dawn's Missing Pages: When stressed to find
the solution to a problem, sometimes all you need
is a little ingenuity and humor

PULLING INTO OUR DRIVEWAY, I looked up. The dingy white skies and the whistle of the wind around the car made me wish I could somehow be transported inside to my warm home, rather than having to get out and unload small children and groceries.

In less than twenty-four hours, a deal I'd been working on for more than six months would finally close. It marked the end of a long process, one that had been unnecessarily time-consuming and at times ridiculously stressful. The deal and its associated details were distracting me significantly from day-to-day experiences with my family. I'd even forgotten to get the ice cream that my husband wanted. It wasn't a big deal, but the fact

I had forgotten it frustrated me; my irritation with myself came across clearly in my phone call to my husband, Chad, when I asked him to pick it up. With the phone call made, I set to the task of unloading.

As I pulled KC out of her seat, I noticed two matted greenish blobs on the lower cushion of her booster seat. As I stared at the seat, an image flashed in my head: Just the day before, I had set her jeans aside in the laundry room, unable to make sense of the odd stain on the back of each of her pant legs.

Now I made the connection.

Herding the children inside, I set the groceries down and grabbed the jeans out of the laundry room. Evidence in hand, I approached KC.

"KC, can you explain what this is?"

She shrugged and quickly downcast her eyes, and her voice dropped. "I dunno."

"KC, did you have green gum in the car?"

My four-year-old, who was paradoxically sneaky and forthcoming, came clean. "Yeeessss. First I took it and hid it in my cup holder. So you wouldn't see, I hid it under my legs."

"After it was chewed?" Somehow the logic escaped me.

"Mmmm-hmmmm." She smiled angelically.

Brilliant.

KC scooted off, happy to be free from the parental "grilling," I'm sure.

Another mess to deal with. The desire to scream and stomp my feet like a child boiled up and I, the somewhat rational adult, pushed it back down. I didn't have time for this. The running list of the work I still had to complete before the night finished played in the back of my brain. Staring at the booster seat cover, I wondered how much a replacement seat cover might run. I knew what I had paid for the jeans; maybe it was easier to throw them away and move forward with the rest of the night. I *really* didn't have time for this.

Furious, I turned toward the trash, grabbing the seat cover and the jeans. Hovering over it, I stopped myself. This was not the way to handle this. Not the message I wanted to send to my kids.

Now I had to search the deep recesses of my brain for what exactly to do with gum on clothing. Peanut butter—or possibly scissors, depending on the severity of the mess—worked for hair. But what the heck do you do with ground-in gum on clothing? My vague recollection was that, as with wax, you make it cold and hard. That way you could sort of break it off the article of clothing.

While I casually put the frozen peas and corn away, I also tossed KC's jeans in the freezer.

Partway through making dinner, assisting with homework, and brokering peace agreements between my two munchkins, I checked on the jeans, hoping for the best. Pulling them out, with knife in hand, I tested my theory.

No luck. The knife pulled at the gum, but it was not ready to break off in frozen chips from my daughter's jeans. Crap.

After stopping to stir my spaghetti sauce on the stove, I tossed the jeans back into the freezer. The level of the issue had escalated. This called for a search of that wonderful source of information and misinformation—the World Wide Web!

As expected, there are many articles about how to get gum off or out of all sorts of things: shoes, cars, clothing, and so on. With a few clicks of my mouse, I was about to become educated.

Gum apparently can be removed from clothing with gasoline. This, however, did not thrill me. I imagined pulling her newly washed jeans out of the washer, only to be met with the smell of gasoline permanently ingrained in the cloth. Then I would be stuck with a four-year-old who reeked like a mechanic; I quickly ruled out *that* solution. Farther down the page, I found references to alcohol and read that gin works especially well.

Not having any gin around, I went for vodka.

Figuring that the base of her car seat might be a better place to test this theory, I pulled it off the structure of the seat and laid it on the counter. If it damaged the seat cover, I didn't really care—no one really sees it on a regular basis. Opening the bottle, I put some on a paper towel and dabbed the gum.

It wasn't enough to really do anything. I would need to pour it directly on the stain, but I didn't want to pour out too much—it was Absolut, after all. Figuring that a shot glass should contain enough vodka to pour on the stain, I poured a shot. As I picked up the glass, I momentarily contemplated drinking it and pouring a second one for the booster seat cover. Again, I regained control and didn't. Not a good lesson for my kids—no matter how stressful the day. But I *was* close.

Making sure the green gooey spot was thoroughly doused in vodka, I grabbed the butcher knife. As I was about to begin scraping the vodka-soaked car seat with my butcher knife, in walked my husband.

Calmly, he passed by, carrying the forgotten half-gallon of French vanilla ice cream, which he had conveniently picked up on the way home. There I stood with a large knife in my hand and an open vodka bottle and a shot glass on the counter. Chad scanned the situation and inhaled, as if he were about to say something. Instead, he closed his mouth and turned toward the freezer. As he opened the freezer door, out fell the jeans.

"Uh. This may be a strange question"—about as strange, I thought, as finding your wife with an open bottle of vodka and wielding a large kitchen knife—"but were you aware that there are jeans in the freezer?"

I started to laugh and put the knife down. Just how crazy did I look? I had almost let the stress of my day get the best of me. Life is going to be stressful and full of challenges, but I wanted to teach my children how to handle them. Thankfully I pulled myself together to solve the problem and didn't act out of anger or frustration, because the night would have been very different for all of us if I hadn't.

After I explained my logic and stirred the sauce a little more, our little experience turned into a science experiment as we tried to figure exactly why alcohol breaks down the gum.

We still don't quite know why it works . . . but we had fun trying to figure it out.

Sometimes parenting requires
one part ingenuity and two parts humor.

He's Gotta Learn

*Dana's Missing Pages: When your heart
tells you to go easy, but you know you can't*

AS WE SAT IN THE DARK, our bedroom lit by only the pale glow of the alarm clock—it read 12:30 a.m.—I heard him, trying to get into the house.

My eyes had adjusted and I could make out the face of my husband, Alan. His jaw was clenched, his muscles tense as he sat beside me in bed.

My sixteen-year-old son, William, was late.

Again.

Only this time it was different. The doors were locked.

Previously when William was late, I would inevitably let him in. He was my only child, and it had been only the two of us for seven years. I had fallen into the pattern of saving William—whether it was letting him in after curfew or bringing his forgotten homework to school, I had slipped into enabling behavior, and now that he was older the years of my saving had resulted in a classic disregard for me and the boundaries that my husband and I sought to establish. It had escalated to the point that we sought the advice of a counselor, who told us to tell William, "The next time you are late, we are locking the doors." I don't think he believed that we—or, more important, I—would actually do it.

What began as a rattling of the front door turned into banging, which grew louder with each passing moment.

I turned to Alan. "What does he think we're going to do, open the door for him?"

Then the doorbell started ringing.

I imagined him out there on the front steps, waiting, hoping that once again we would bend our rules and open the door.

The doorbell rang several times more.

My attempts to remain calm and relaxed were futile. Part of me wanted to run down and pull my gangly, teenaged "baby" inside, if for no other reason than I merely wanted the doorbell ringing to stop. The other half of me knew this was not the solution.

Finally it was quiet, except for the continuous chirp of the crickets. Thankfully it was a summer night and I didn't have to worry that William was cold. There was movement outside; I heard him walking away. Although I did not know where he was going, my gut told me he was probably searching for another window or door that might be open and might offer him a way in.

Ten minutes passed and there was nothing.

"Alan, where do you think he is?"

"I don't know. He knew the rules. Maybe he went to Hugh's house; it's within walking distance. Regardless, we need to get some sleep. When he comes home in the morning we'll discuss this with him. Until then, there's nothing more we can do."

Alan slid down into bed, pulled the covers up, and turned his back to me; this conversation was over and he intended to go to sleep. Although I knew what Alan said was true, I couldn't rest.

Adjusting my pillow, I heard footsteps. I could clearly make out the stealthy clomp of size fourteen sneakers, squeaking on my wood floors.

"Alan! I think he's in the house."

Alan sat upright. The tension returned to his face. "But there's no way he could've gotten in."

Our whispered discussion was interrupted by the sound of the wood stairs creaking. William had definitely made it inside. The mixture of relief, curiosity, and astonishment hit me. Alan's voice echoed my thoughts. "I can't believe he got in!"

Pushing the covers back, Alan swung his legs over the side of the bed and made his way to our bedroom door. I wasn't far behind.

Simultaneously opening our bedroom door and flipping on the hall light switch, we walked down the hall and into William's room, which he had just entered.

William froze. Underneath his shaggy blond hair I saw his eyes large and round, his mouth gaping. It reminded me of the times that I caught him sneaking cookies as a little boy.

"William. Would you care to tell us how you got in?" I asked.

"Uh, no. I'm not telling you." The gaping mouth tightened.

"Oh, yes, you are. That was not a question, William. Tell us how you got in," Alan said.

"If I tell you how I got in, then I can't use it again."

I didn't know whether I was angry or not. In part I was impressed with his creativity, but that feeling was soon brushed aside and replaced with anger and frustration. William was always pushing the rules. I wished that just once, he would listen and respect the boundaries we tried to set.

"William, you need to tell us. We set rules, and you

constantly disrespect them. You need to tell us how you got in," I said.

William's eyes were downcast. He was contemplating his next move.

"Well, what's it gonna be, William?" I tried in vain to make eye contact.

Still, William was silent. He shifted his weight and finally spoke. "I came in through the sliding glass door."

This didn't make any sense. The sliding glass door was on the second floor with a safety barrier up against it, because there was almost a story between the door and the ground below.

"How did you reach the door?" I wanted to know.

"I used the firewood stacked up against the house, and then pulled myself up. The door was left open, so I came in."

Although relieved he was being honest with us—and I admit I was impressed with his ingenuity—the incident highlighted something I had not wanted to face.

When William wanted something badly enough, he would move mountains to make it happen. But that same motivation did not apply when it came to doing the things he should do—like keeping rules and respecting his parents.

I was upset it had reached this point; nothing had changed. I felt as if I had failed as a parent; more than that, I was hurt by his disrespect for us, for our boundaries. With all the strength I had at that late hour, I turned to my son and said, "William, you need to know that you won't have this opportunity again. We will go through the house, checking and locking all of the windows and doors. Don't bother trying to break in. If you're late, then you will simply have to find someplace other than inside this house to sleep."

William peered back at me, tossed his hair back, and said, "Sure, Mom, whatever. Soon enough I will be out of here and on my own and it won't matter anymore."

With my head cocked to the side and my eyes narrowed, I spoke in a measured voice to him. "You have no idea what it takes to live on your own with no safety net."

His words held blatant disregard and reflected years in which I had said one thing but not followed through. He thought he knew what it meant to be independent but really had no idea. When he forgot a school assignment, he knew he could call and I would run it to him. In my attempts to provide for him, to help make him successful, I often overlooked the very boundaries I had set. In so doing, I had created an environment in which my son had little appreciation for boundaries and consequences—something that he would soon run into in the real world.

Alan and I went back to our bedroom, defeated by our thwarted attempts to define and hold our boundaries. I knew for William's sake, and mine, that I needed to hold true to my word.

Like any parent, I would never want him in an unsafe position. I was somewhat comforted by the fact that I knew that William had enough sense to find a safe place to sleep and that he'd come back in the morning. It was time I let him start experiencing true consequences for his behavior, otherwise he was never going to be able to learn to live on his own.

After that night William continued to violate curfew, but he started asking his friends to wait to see if he could get into the house. When he couldn't, he would simply drive away with them and stay somewhere else. Eventually, if it was past curfew, he stopped trying to get into the house, opting to staying at a friend's house instead.

Once high school was finished, William left, determined to live on his own. I remember when he announced that he was moving out. By that point I had learned to let go, but I wondered if he had absorbed any of the lessons I had tried to teach him. Alan and I didn't fight him and his decision to leave, and I wondered if I had done the right thing.

A few months later, friends told me that William had been counseling their daughter, who was having similar issues with her parents—our friends. During the conversation they overheard William telling her, "My mom was right—you have no idea what it takes to live on your own." Hearing that, I thought maybe he did "get it" after all, and I realized sometimes you need to ignore your heart to do what is best for your child.

Being too lenient, whether it is under the guise of trying to protect the child or not, doesn't allow them to learn important lessons about self-discipline. Children desperately need to learn these tough lessons to survive in this difficult world.

Breaking the Ties that Bind

*Rachel's Missing Pages: When you need
to be bold and let go of the past*

"CAN YOU STATE THE NAME of the biological father?"

"Yes, Your Honor. His name is Stephen Donovan." I paused and stole a look at Aiden. His eight-year-old frame looked smaller within the confines of the large, wood-paneled courtroom.

The judge peered at me over his bifocals. "Have you received any support from Mr. Donovan since the child's birth?"

"No, Your Honor, I have not."

"Please state your request for the biological father."

I looked down briefly at my hands. Despite being clenched, they shook, rippling the flowered pattern of my skirt. Inhaling a long, deep breath, I visualized stillness. Acutely aware that Aiden and Jason, my husband, were behind me, with Aiden watching my every move, I could not let him see me falter. It was time that Aiden heard the truth about his father, a truth kept secret for all these years.

For as long as Aiden had been alive, I had shielded him from the details of his absent, alcoholic father. Now, in a room full of people, I was speaking out loud all of the details I had worked for years to conceal. I spoke of the absent years, the alcoholic binges, and the refusal to support or want to have anything to do with our son. Although aware that parenting was about tough choices, I was unprepared for how guilty I felt: not about my choice, but about my inability to spare my son from enduring this ordeal. Aiden had known that his father was absent, but over the years I had compensated for it, dancing around the fact that his father loved the bottle more than his own son. Now he was hearing me speak the brutal truth for the first time.

"I am requesting that his parental rights be terminated and that my son, Aiden, be adopted by my husband, Jason Bowers." With those words, I turned and looked behind me.

Jason was smiling, his arm protectively around Aiden. Aiden's eyes quietly scanned the room, taking in all the players, his face a mixture of curiosity and anxiousness. Behind him sat all of our family, including the Bowers family—now Aiden's new family.

When I glanced back at the judge, he was signing the documents spread out before him.

With the stroke of a pen, the judge erased all of Aiden's history. As far as the world was concerned he was a Bowers, and Jason was his father.

The conclusion of the hearing brought many tears, broad smiles, and hugs amid the family gathered for the event. Standing there I watched as they surrounded Aiden, enveloping him with their love. He returned their hugs, a smile extending the length of his face. I stood back from them, remembering when this journey began.

From the time I met Jason, I had been cautious about his interaction with Aiden, who was only three years old. Five months of dating went by before they even met. Over time, they became closer and went on "boys only" camping trips, to give them an opportunity to deepen their relationship.

When Jason and I finally approached the idea of getting married, we investigated ways to ensure that Aiden felt a part of the process. Our marriage ceremony was a "family" ceremony, which included Aiden accepting Jason into our lives. As the years progressed, Aiden began to call Jason "Dad."

I thought I had done everything right.

Then Jason and I conceived. Right before Aiden's third grade year, and after the baby had been born, we moved from the apartment that Aiden and I had shared from the time he was an infant. Our new house was in a neighboring state, in an area we thought would be better for raising our two children. It seemed that my life had settled into a new and exciting course.

But toward the end of that fall, as the holiday break approached, we noticed a shift in Aiden. Papers were coming home filled with errors on material that we knew was review for him. It was clear something was bothering him, but attempts at uncovering what it was yielded nothing but clamped jaws and lack of eye contact. Determined to get to the bottom of the shift in his demeanor and grades, we sat him down one night.

"Aiden, what's going on? Is something bothering you?"

His eyes fell to the floor, and he gave a little shrug. "I dunno."

Gently I lifted his head up, revealing his face. There was a pang in my heart when I saw that Aiden's eyes were filled with tears. "I don't wanna have to leave our new home with Dad and go back to the apartment without him."

"What? Why would we do that, honey?"

"I dunno. Because I don't like my school and if I had to change, it would mean leaving here and leaving Dad."

Jason and I looked at each other in stunned silence. Regardless of his school problems, there was a bigger issue at play if he thought moving would necessarily mean splitting up the family. We had missed something.

Later, when Aiden was in bed, we talked it through. We could only conclude that, despite our best efforts, Aiden still did not feel he belonged. He didn't feel a part of this family and as such could at any time be separated from it.

I didn't choose to raise my son without his biological father, Stephen. Instead, his father had checked out years ago. Given Stephen's propensity for alcoholic binges, his absence allowed me to shield Aiden from the alcohol-fueled escapades. However, there were still moments when I wondered if I could have done something better or differently so that Aiden wouldn't have had all those years without a dad. Regardless, I couldn't change the fact that my son was scarred by my ex's abandonment.

Just when I thought I had done everything I could, bringing a wonderful, stable new man into our lives, I discovered it was not enough to heal that wounded place inside my son. Something more needed to be done, and I simply didn't know at that time what it was.

It was Jason who actually approached me about formally adopting Aiden. The love he had shown for my son was evident more than ever in his immediate willingness to take on this legal role. Feelings of appreciation were soon mixed with anxiety—anxiety related to Aiden's reaction and to what the adoption process would unearth.

We had moved on to a new normal in which the absence of Aiden's father was becoming less noticeable as Jason assumed more of the fatherly duties. Moving through the lengthy adoption process had the possibility for opening up memories and wounds long buried and destroying what little peace and stability Aiden now had.

There would be legal attempts to find and locate Stephen, as required as part of the process. I anticipated that these attempts would fail, which would facilitate the adoption process and at the same time act as a searing reminder that Aiden's father *simply didn't want his son.* If the efforts to locate Stephen were successful, then what? If Stephen made a mediocre attempt to reach out to Aiden and then vanished again, how would Aiden take it? Could Aiden return to even where he was right now? How would I support and protect him then? The process alone was an emotional minefield.

Despite the possible risks, Jason and I determined that moving forward with the adoption was the right thing to do. There was one more thing that needed to be done; we needed to ask Aiden what he wanted.

It was a Saturday and we had spent the day hiking. Returning home, we feasted on grilled hamburgers and baked steak fries— Aiden's favorite. Our bellies full, we spread out in the living room. The day had been a good one, and it was the perfect time to approach Aiden.

"Aiden, Jason and I have been talking and . . ."

Jason interrupted me. "I'd like to adopt you so I can be your father in *all ways.*" Searching Aiden's face for a response, he added, "Would you like that?"

Aiden's eyes first met Jason's and then sought reassurance from mine. A smile spread across his face. Turning toward Jason, he asked, "Would I have your last name?"

I nodded for Jason to reply. "Yup, and you can pick a new middle name too if you want," Jason said.

"Yeah, that would be cool. I'd like that. Um, can I pick *any* middle name?"

I could see the wheels turning in his head as he glanced at the stack of wrestling trading cards sitting on the wooden coffee table. His fondness for professional wrestling could add a whole new dimension to the middle name choice. Hugging him, I said, "Within reason, Aiden."

That was more than a year ago.

Now, in the courtroom, I closed my eyes, took a deep breath, and smiled. Opening them again, I looked upon the joy and love surrounding my son. The adoption was complete; Jason was now Aiden's dad in every sense.

As the crowd of family and close friends separated from Aiden, I looked at him, holding Jason's hand, smiling. In that moment I relished the sweetness of it all. Despite the anxiety I had had, I knew we had made the right decision.

Sometimes, to get to the future, we and our children need to face hard truths. When in doubt, move forward as boldly as you can.

Color-Blind

*Heather's Missing Pages: When your child faces
prejudice or rejection*

THE WARM SEPTEMBER SUN streamed in through the window—
the perfect day for my three kids to enjoy the park—even if it
was without me. I had walked my children around to the park,
located behind our row of townhomes, and had left the older
boys with strict instructions to look after their sister. Although
I wanted to join them, I was thankful that my boys, now thirteen and eleven, could look after Morgan, who had just turned
seven years old, because the mountains of laundry demanded my
immediate attention.

Puttering around the house, I worked on the laundry,
grateful that instead of my boisterous children, all I heard was
the hum of the washer and dryer. I soaked in the momentary,
relative quiet their absence granted me.

That moment quickly left me when I heard the front door open and slam shut. Loud angry sobbing echoed from the foyer. It was my daughter, Morgan.

Racing downstairs, I met her as she kicked off her shoes. Surveying her body for any obvious signs of injury, I couldn't find the source of the ailment. Although her chest was heaving with sobs, there were no signs of outward damage, which probably meant that her feelings were hurt.

I pulled her toward me, smoothed her hair, and held her tight. "Honey, what's wrong?"

Her body shook with sobs. "They . . . called me . . . a . . . little black girl!" With that, she abandoned what was left of her reserve and continued to cry. All I managed to do was stand there, holding her, mystified.

"Breathe, baby. Who said this?"

With her face buried in my stomach, I heard her muffled response. "The kids on the swings."

When I initially walked the kids down to the park, there were only three other children there—three boys. I surmised that these were the same kids that she was referring to. More than that, I could tell by her intense response that calling her "little black girl" was not just an observation but a put-down.

I imagined they were still there, too, and probably not very far from where my two sons, Pierce and Donovan, were still playing kickball.

The racial issue was nothing new to us. We are a biracial family. I am white, my partner is not. The coloring and features of our children vary as much as their personalities. The oldest child, Donovan, has dark brown hair and eyes and a complexion that often has him mistaken for being Puerto Rican. Pierce is extremely fair like me, with blond hair and blue eyes. Morgan has the coffee-with-cream complexion of her father but startlingly blue eyes.

Although race had come up before with the boys, it was different. Donovan, while studying the Civil War, had once remarked that because of his skin color he might have been able to avoid the side door—or slave door—of a house. Pierce, after learning about color mixing in art class, had come home and declared that he was simply gray—essentially, a mix of black and white. Both of them simply accepted that they were a mix, similar to variations in eye or hair color. Neither had ever hung a label on who they were.

We have always taught our children that they are loved for who they are, for their unique spirits and talents. We never wanted them to be put into one category for fear they might use it as a means to limit their own growth and development. Therefore it was understandable why Morgan was this upset by being slapped with a label.

Holding her in my arms, I wished I could change this world in which everyone has to be categorized or labeled. But this kind of change takes time—a lot of time. Although my children's generation is better than mine was, the reality is that we as a society like to label people. Maybe—trying to be positive about it—as a way of making order out of chaos. Regardless, it's still labeling and certainly not productive. In fact, it reduces and strips away all that makes each of us unique, bunching us instead into generic groups.

This is what happened to my girl, whose sobs were now abating. She felt reduced to simply being a little black girl.

Now the precise thing I had avoided, labeling anyone because of race, had to be explained to my daughter. By me, her white mother—someone who had rarely experienced being labeled anything.

I pulled Morgan from me and said, "Sweetie, I'd like to talk to you about this, but I need you to calm down first. Deep breaths, Morgan. Deep breaths."

Holding her at arm's length, I practiced deep breaths with her until she was calm. Until she was, she wouldn't really hear what I was about to say next.

"Morgan, what color is Mommy's skin?"

"Light."

"What about Daddy?"

"Darker."

"Morgan, you are the perfect blend of both of us."

Morgan eyed me with a studious expression on her face. She wasn't sure if she understood where I was going, or if this would make her feel better. *Switch gears*, I thought.

"Morgan, I'm Irish—right?"

She rolled her eyes, furrowed her brow, and responded, "Yeaaaahhhh."

"I am what people would classify as white, and your dad is black . . . but really we are all the same."

Again, the dubious look.

"Morgan, what color was Grandma?"

"Darker than Daddy."

"She would be considered black, right?"

"Yes."

"She was a neat lady, right?"

"Yeah." A small light of recognition brightened her eyes. She had loved her grandmother and had looked up to her.

"You are partially black and partially white, but most important, you are the perfect mix of us—your family, who loves you and who you love. We are good to each other, and we are good people. And the fact that our skins are different colors is part of what makes us unique—you included."

Holding her a little tighter, I continued. "The little boys weren't entirely wrong. Your skin is dark, but the way they look at that isn't right."

Morgan turned her head up toward mine; I saw the tears

fading and a calmness setting in.

"So what do I do if they call me that again? What do I say?"

"You say what you want to. Tell them you're a perfect mix and that you're proud that you are. You know who you are, so what they say doesn't really matter."

Luckily that answer seemed to work—for the moment. Because Morgan comes from such a blended family, I know that she will have other experiences as she grows up. I know that she will witness firsthand prejudices that just don't seem fair . . . and really aren't.

For now, as a parent in a biracial family, I hope to get through moments like this—challenges to us as human beings with different skin colors—until there is a day when the color of your skin is irrelevant.

As irrelevant as the color of your eyes . . . whoever you may be, reading these words.

We need to teach our children to trust that each possesses the perfect balance, that no one person is better than another. That is what makes each child special. Only we can define the value of a label.

And This Too Shall Pass

*Natalie's Missing Pages: When you're asked
to bear a heavy loss*

AS MY HUSBAND, MARK, drove us home from Easter mass, our older daughters' laughter and chatter filled the car's backseat. This was then accompanied by a belly giggle that erupted from two-year-old Elsa, the youngest by nine years. Ideally all six of our children would have been at mass together, but Joe was away and our other two sons were at home still sleeping off their Saturday night.

Elsa's giggles were interrupted by the sound of my cell phone ringing in my purse. I flipped it open and plugged my left ear in a vain attempt to hear what my son Daniel was saying.

"Mom? Hey, the Navy called. They want to speak to you or Dad about Joe." The strain in Daniel's voice spoke volumes—he was worried. Mark's eyes briefly left the road as he glanced at me.

Somehow he knew something was wrong.

The Navy. Both my husband, Mark, and I had served, and our middle son, Joe, was currently serving. Getting a call at home was not ideal, but if they were only calling, it probably meant that he had been injured in some way. Not great . . . but I knew it could be far worse.

"Thanks, Danny. We're almost home from church. We'll call them when we get in."

Arriving back at the house, I directed the girls outside toward the gardens and followed them. I hoped the diversion would give Mark the quiet space he needed to return the Navy's call.

A few minutes later, I looked up to see Mark standing at the French doors, silently watching us. Goose bumps spread across my skin with the realization that this had to be more than an injury. From Mark's facial expression, I knew something was terribly wrong.

"Emmie, can you watch the girls?" I said to our older daughter. "I need to talk to Dad for a second."

"Okay, Mom."

Reaching the door, Mark motioned toward the den, his sanctuary. Soon after he closed the French doors, I was struck by the fragrance of Easter lilies that still hung on our clothes. Sitting across from Mark, I took a deep breath.

"Mark, what's wrong?"

"Joe is missing."

"What do you mean, missing? You don't just go missing on a ship."

"That's just it. There was an early morning training exercise, and he was accidentally knocked overboard. They can't find him."

I stared at my husband while my world spun out of control. Taking it all in, I closed my eyes, but all I saw were Joe's perpetually smiling, green ones in return. My stomach churned; I wondered if I was going to be sick.

Instead, my attention was riveted on Mark. He had already lost his first wife, who was pregnant with a child, in an accident. The thought that he might lose another child was unbearable. Mark turned away from me, tears flowing down his cheeks.

My mouth went dry and I breathed in a pain that traveled down my throat and into my chest. It was like someone had reached inside my chest and ripped my heart into pieces. My sense of reality faded; I felt as if I were floating above this nightmare and in it at the same time. The cries I heard coming out of the woman who had collapsed in the chair seemed to come from someone else. The warmth of Mark's arms around me brought me back into my own body. It was then I realized the cries I heard were my own.

His eyes were red. But other than that, he had erased all trace of his tears.

Standing up, he said, "We need to tell the other kids."

Barely nodding, I reached for the tissues. I blotted my eyes in a feeble attempt to mask the emotions pouring from them. He was right. We had to do this, and we had to be strong . . . for them. However, my shaking hand on the den door indicated otherwise.

We assembled the three girls and two boys in the family room. As a large family, we occasionally had family meetings, but never one like this. They gathered on the sofas and looked at the two of us sitting together, hand in hand, on the ottoman. I gazed at their faces, then down to the creases in my skirt; I then heard Mark's voice as he repeated the news of Joe's disappearance to the kids.

Emmie started to cry first. Then Catheryn. Both Daniel and James sat with their heads down and their faces obscured from my view, sobbing. Elsa sat among her wooden blocks and studied the sadness surrounding her, holding a block suspended in the air, undecided as to whether she should add to her ever-growing tower or stop building all together. Emmie's continued cries made the decision for Elsa. The sorrow too much to take, Elsa ran toward me and buried her face in my chest.

Mark continued, "They're going to keep looking for him."

Jumping in, I added, "Guys, we can't give up hope. Joe needs us to believe he is okay and will be found. He needs our prayers." Putting Elsa on my knee, I reached toward Mark's hand and then Emmie's, and they reached out their hands, until we were all standing there in a circle, barely whispering, "Our Father, who art in Heaven . . ."

I don't remember much about the next several days. Each day I got up and went through the motions, losing myself in the mundane, cleaning every surface of my house. I spent hours with a brush on the kitchen floor, methodically removing the grime, while Elsa napped. I could control the dirt; it was the only thing I could control.

Occasionally, the numbness gave way to crying, and I hoped those moments manifested only when my children weren't around. I wanted to be the face of hope for them, even if I carried little in my heart.

Thankfully, my brothers, who were officers in the Navy, had joined the search. They were there doing what I couldn't do, which was to search for my son.

My brothers called first, before the "official" visit from the Navy—Joe's body had been found. It was a call that we'd expected, but equally hoped would never come. After hanging up the phone, Mark and I remained there in the den, holding each other as if somehow that action might mitigate some of the pain between us.

Sitting in the den, the same one we'd sat in three days before, we prepared to do one last thing for our son. Our eyes still swollen and red, we began discussing the logistics of bringing Joe home and planning his funeral—things that parents hope they will never have to deal with. Thankfully, our children were outside and not immediate witnesses to our grief.

When we told the children Joe was missing, it was just that . . . he was missing. Maybe he was dead, but we still held out hope. Knowing that he was truly gone from us was something else. Mark had suffered the loss of his wife and unborn child, but I had not gone through this type of tremendous loss before and certainly not as a mother. I needed support from the only person I knew who had been there *herself*, as a mother. I called my mom, who lost her son, my brother Neil, when I was growing up.

"Mom, I don't know what to say. I don't know if I can bear this loss *and* watch my kids suffer through their grief, too. I wish I could protect them from this."

I was met with silence.

"Mom, are you still there? What should I do?"

The silence continued for a moment more. Perhaps my mother was trying to gather her thoughts, because I would not soon forget what she said next.

"Natalie, sometimes you have to realize that everything is unfolding as it should be. As strange as it may sound, you are in a much better position than most in understanding what your children are going through. In losing your brother, you are able to understand your children's grief. You can no more protect them than I could protect you. You have to rest in the belief that this experience is being given to each of them for a reason."

At first her words stung. But they were the words of some-one from a different generation who had witnessed wars; more important, my mother knew what it was like to lose a child and still have to go on for her family. I wanted to argue with her. I wanted to say that this *reason* did nothing to ease the terrible ache in my heart or the intense desire to crawl into bed and escape it all. I opened my mouth to reply . . . but didn't.

In that moment, I also realized I was partially comforted by the thought that there *might* be a reason for all of this. Although Joe's death was senseless, my ability to understand my children's loss gave me a brief sense of purpose. Yet . . . how was I going to console my children or make their childhood a happy place ever again, when I felt this much sadness? My jumbled thoughts were interrupted by the sound of my mother's voice.

"A part of you will always be tied to Joe. That part can and will grieve for him. But you need to reserve and direct the rest of your energies toward Mark and the remaining children. To be there to support them through this sadness, but more important, to be actively engaged and *present* for them as they continue to live."

When we had finished talking, I hung up the phone and sat there for a moment, thinking back to when my brother Neil died. I remembered feeling incredibly sad, but in that sadness, life continued and with it happy memories as well. I realized that both good times and bad times pass. *It all passes*, I thought. *All of it.*

Standing on the wisdom that came from my mother's lived experience, I thought, *She's right.* Life is best lived in the present, because all too quickly every moment and memory fades, replaced by new ones. If we hold on to any experience, bad or good, it will block what is to come.

Later we gathered the children again in the family room, each of us resuming our places. Even before we spoke, they saw the sadness in our eyes and silently the tears began to cascade freely down their faces.

In one of the days following the funeral, I heard Elsa's belly giggles coming from the den. I stood there for several minutes and watched Mark smile for the first time since that dreaded call, delighting in Elsa's silliness. I wanted to soak the moment up . . . because I knew, much like Joe's passing, this moment too would pass. I was learning the wisdom of letting go and living in each present moment.

This too shall pass. Clinging to memories can block the ability to create new ones—whether they be bad or good. Live life in the present and enjoy and value the people still in it.

Competing for Mommy Time

Anna's Missing Pages: When you feel like you don't have anything left to give

"MIJO!" I SAID, with as much enthusiasm as I could muster as I pushed open the door to his classroom at the daycare center.

Mateo, my three-year-old son, looked up from coloring at his table and stared at me with his enormous brown eyes. A smile spread across his face. "Maaaaa-maaa!"

In an instant he had pushed the chair back, run across the room, and jumped into my arms, cradling my face in his small hands. Pressing his forehead against mine, he placed a gentle butterfly kiss on my nose. I smiled in return and placed him back on the linoleum.

"Mamma, we did a lot today. I played with Thomas the Tank Engine and built a castle with blocks and . . ." Mateo went on and on, regaling me with tales of his day.

"That's great, honey! Now let's get going!" I said, grabbing his coat and lunchbox out of his cubby. I was desperately trying to move the process along so that we could get home and I might be able stop running around for a moment.

Exiting the preschool and then again in the car, I learned of the dragons he slayed and the food he ate. I learned about *everything*. Part of me was so excited to hear his little voice . . . and yet I felt a twinge of guilt.

After a long, intense day, a big part of me longed for silence. Peace.

As we pulled into our driveway, dread peppered with guilt continued to rise. I knew that the minute we got in the door, Mateo would want me to play with him. It was the last thing I felt like doing after working eight hours as an ICU nurse.

Before I had the opportunity to put my keys down, it began.

"Mamma! Let's play. Whaddaya wanna play, Mamma? Want to play blocks?" Mateo's expectant face was turned up toward mine, beaming, full of energy. I looked at him and wished I had his energy and not the fatigue that permeated my body after a long day at work.

"In a minute, Mateo. I have to put these things down. Then Mommy would like to sit a minute and look through the mail to see if anything important came. Okay?"

The air deflated out of Mateo, and his shoulders sagged a little. I knew I had done that to him, that all he wanted was me. But I also knew I needed a moment to breathe at the end of the day. Taking care of patients all day was draining before I became a mother. Now it felt like everyone, including my son, needed my full attention at all times and there was never any time for me to recharge.

After getting a glass of water, I sat on the sofa and began slowly sorting through the mail I had set down on the coffee table. Mateo ran behind me, making a whirling noise as his toy plane soared through the air. Then I heard him bring the plane in for a landing near his toy bin.

Just as a tiny bit of calm was returning, Mateo pushed his way in between me and the stack of mail. He knocked over my glass of water, leaving the stack a soggy mess.

"Mateo! *Dios mio!*" I yelled. The clipped words escaped my mouth before I could stop them. "What have you done?"

His face fell. My words had stung. Mateo's little frame deflated and tears flooded into his eyes.

"I'm sorry, Mamma. I was just tryin' to see if there was any mail for me." His small voice echoed off the tile floor and the walls around us.

Pulling him toward me, I hugged him and buried my face into his mass of dark brown hair.

I hadn't imagined it would be this hard when I went back to work six months ago. I don't know what I'd imagined, but I had not anticipated being this drained. Consequently, there was precious little of me left for my child. I knew he was three and couldn't possibly understand; it was obvious that all he wanted was a little time from me. But after giving so much of myself all day to patients, I also knew that I had remarkably little left for him—much less myself.

"Mateo, I'm sorry I snapped at you. It's just, well . . . I'm tired. I love you, *mijo*, and I know it was an accident. Okay?"

Mateo looked back at me. His eyes betrayed his emotions, and I knew he seriously doubted that it was *okay*.

Guilt crept up from my stomach and into my throat, causing it to tighten. I had caused my son to doubt that I loved and valued him—I needed to fix this. But at the moment I didn't know how.

Clean up the mess, was all that I could think to do. *He only wants a moment of your time. A moment with you.*

I gathered myself, pushing the anger and guilt back down. Then I kissed him, smiled, and threw a hand towel on the pile of soggy bills.

I grabbed his hand as we walked away from the mess and I asked, "What do you want to build, *mi niño*?"

The light began to expand in his eyes, and a smile once again spread across his face. I knew I couldn't merely offer him a kiss and hope that he would give me time to regroup. It wasn't realistic or fair. This constant struggle wasn't healthy for either of us. I needed to offer him something more than a kiss and the attitude that said, *Mommy's tired from working all day. Please go play and leave me alone.*

I needed to offer him a bit of myself.

As Mateo and I played with his blocks on the area rug on the living room floor, I thought through my situation. As tired as I was each day, as much as I gave to other people, I needed to reserve a piece of me for simply being present for him. I needed to figure out a way that we could spend time together, but also have some way for me to restore some of the energy lost in treating patients.

The next day during my lunch break, I went to the craft store and bought a variety of crafts and activities that Mateo could do with limited supervision. When we returned that evening, I put my plan into action. Arriving at home, I put everything down and focused all of my attention on Mateo for the first thirty minutes after walking in the door. He had not had me all day, and I knew he needed me. He needed that time.

But once it was over, it was time for our talk. I called him into the kitchen where I was seated at the table.

"*Mijo.*"

"Yes, Mamma?"

"You know how we share our toys?"

"Mmmm-hmmm."

"Well, doing things together and the time you spend with someone is kinda like that. Sometimes we need to share our time, as we would share a toy. We just spent time doing something together that you wanted, and now, we are each going to spend some time doing our own things—near each other, but separately."

From across the table I couldn't tell if he was retaining anything I said. Instead, he focused on the columns of new Play-Doh stacked carefully in colorful towers in front of me. Within seconds after I slid it over, Mateo had eased into a seat and was fully engrossed.

There was a silence and contentment I had not witnessed since I had gone back to work. My thirty-minute "offering" had done its work.

With that, I picked up the paper and read. Occasionally I found myself looking over at Mateo and the royal-blue and hot-pink blobs he was creating, but he kept himself occupied, and I was able to relax.

I had finally discovered a way to decompress from the day and still be near my son. It wasn't perfect, but it was something that met both of our needs. The guilt was removed and I was given the critical time I needed to regenerate myself. Feeling reinvigorated, I found myself happier and honestly thought I would be able to give more of myself to my son than I would have had we continued in the pattern we were in before.

As a parent you struggle between being there for your child and allowing time for yourself. It's not just okay to give yourself a break; it's important to do so. Sometimes it requires creativity, but you need to make the time and space for you and your child. You will have more energy and more to give to your child if you do, and both of your needs will be better met.

Unlucky Luck

*Ed's Missing Pages: When the lesson
you're trying to teach misses the mark*

THE DOOR TO BOB'S Beer, Bait and Booze eased open, the old bells sounding a familiar jingle as they slid across the glass.

"Hey, Ed."

"Hey, Deacon."

It was a familiar interchange that had changed little in the years I'd been coming here. Although I had finally graduated to "Ed," an occasional "Eddie" still slipped out.

"Who did ya bring with you? This big boy can't be little Grayson! You know, Eddie, he looks like you did at that age."

I saw my son stand a little bit taller with the compliment. *Yep*, I thought, *he does look a lot like I did at eight. We have the same dirty blond hair and green eyes muddied with flecks of brown, which makes it hard to tell if they're green or hazel.*

As I looked around the store, I remembered coming to Bob's when I was Grayson's age. It was like the store was frozen in time, except the shelves, previously loaded with dusty cans, were now filled with a broad array of boutique beers and wines. By the door was a scratch-ticket lottery machine where the local papers used to be stocked.

"Ed, we have some of that Flying Dog beer that you like." Deacon nodded his head toward the bank of refrigerators near the back of the store. "Folks say it that it goes with barbecue real well. I dunno, I haven't had it yet, but that's what they say."

As I walked toward the back, Grayson stayed up by the front with Deacon. I heard snippets of their conversation, which inevitably turned toward fishing. Grabbing a six-pack, I returned to the front of the store just in time to find Grayson over by the brightly lit, scratch-off lottery ticket machine.

Grayson is an inquisitive boy who has always wanted to know and understand everything; therefore I was not surprised when he grabbed my hand and demanded to know, "Hey, Dad, what's this?"

"That's a lottery machine that sells scratch-off tickets. People buy the tickets and then scratch off different areas on them in hopes that they'll win a prize, or money."

I saw the wheels turning in his head. I almost never play the lottery, in any way, shape, or form. It's just not where I ever have wanted to put my money. Yet time and again you see people contributing their hard-earned dollars for a nominal payout—paying for the hope that this will be their big day, the day they are the big winner. It's glaringly obvious, to me at least, who the winners actually are.

"Dad, can I play? I have two dollars with me."

"Sorry, buddy, you have to be an adult to play."

"Oh." His voice trailed off, and his shoulders dropped with disappointment.

Then he lifted his head and his eyes lit up; I knew what was coming next. "Dad, could *you* play for me?"

Deacon was leaning back behind the counter with his arms crossed, grinning, watching the interchange. He was studying both of us, trying to stifle the chuckle.

"Eddie, are you gonna play for the boy?"

My head turned toward him, and I returned a look that clearly indicated I did not appreciate his "help" in this matter. Standing there, I genuinely did not know what to do. I knew I didn't like feeding into this system, which preys largely on a group of people who can't afford to blow portions of their paycheck each week on the possibility of winning. Occasionally they do win a few dollars here and there—just enough to feed the obsession that they could possibly win the big prize. Then that money, which would probably be better spent on fundamental things like food and rent, is lost and the cycle repeats.

These weightier social issues and implications would have to wait until Grayson was older. Instead, it occurred to me that this was a fantastic opportunity to teach my son a valuable life lesson. As a parent, I much prefer using experiences that I can turn into lessons rather than simply discussing them.

"Grayson," I asked, "what did you have to do to earn those dollars?"

"I helped wash your car, Dad."

"And it took you a couple of hours, right? Those were hours that you could have spent playing in the backyard or with your friends, right?"

"Yeah."

"You worked hard to earn that money and gave up your time to do it. If you have me buy a lottery ticket with it, you could lose that money entirely. It's the chance you take. Do you see this sign?" I asked, pointing to the machine. "It tells you the chances for this dollar game. What does it say?"

"It says, 'Overall Odds 1:4.88,' and then it lists a bunch of prizes we could win with numbers next to them. Dad! We could win as much as six thousand dollars!"

This was not going as expected.

"Yeah, buddy, we could. But look at the numbers next to it. It says 1 in 240,000. That means, for every 240,000 tickets sold, only one would win that six thousand dollars. Do you know what a tiny chance we have of winning?"

"Oh." Grayson's face dropped. But, ever the optimist, he looked back up, handed me his dollar, and said, "Dad, I want you to try."

I couldn't understand why he wanted to continue. I'd done my best to dump cold water on this foolishness. But I figured it was a fitting way to learn a tough lesson, and it was better that he learned it now.

I took his money, fed it into the machine, and selected a ticket. We brought it over to the counter and I handed Grayson a nickel to use to scratch off the mystery silver coating.

As the coating flaked away, it revealed "$40."

"Try again," Grayson said, pointing to another silver spot.

"$40" came up again.

As the silver coating sloughed off the numbers one by one, my anticipated satisfaction at proving my point was replaced by sheer amazement.

"DAD!" Grayson was jumping up and down. "We won forty dollars!"

Deacon put his hand over his face in an effort to veil the grin hiding behind it. I heard a laugh, which Deacon quickly attempted to disguise as a cough as he turned from me. All I could think was, *Are you kidding me?* My efforts to teach a positive life lesson had utterly gone wrong.

Still holding on to the joy of his winnings, Grayson beamed at me. "Dad, this is great. We should do this all the time!"

"Well, Grayson," I said, chagrined, "I can't believe it. You were lucky this time. This probably won't happen again. You should consider this like 'found money' and we should put all but maybe five dollars of it into the bank."

We left Bob's a little richer and in some ways, the important ways, a little poorer.

The life lesson I had wanted to teach my son would have to wait for another day.

Parenting often requires us to think on our feet, to try to turn moments into teachable ones for our children. But even when you think you've got it, you still need to be prepared for things to backfire. Trust that another opportunity will come along to teach that important life lesson.

Healthy Curiosity, Healthy Body Image

Geni's Missing Pages: When your child is curious about her body

"BYE, SUZY! THANKS FOR coming over!" I shouted while my seven-year-old daughter, Ella, and I waved good-bye to her friend and her mother as they pulled away down our street.

Closing the door, I set about straightening the house and continuing the laundry. With a freshly folded pile of laundry in hand, I walked up the stairs and into my room to put it away. Easing the drawer of my dresser in, I turned to walk back downstairs. To the right of our bedroom door was a desk, and on it our house computer.

The computer screen was off. We always left the screen on—this was strange.

Sitting down at the desk, I turned the screen back on and

moved the mouse around to wake the computer up from being in sleep mode. The monitor burst into life and a purple screen stared back at me. A completely purple screen for Yahoo? That's new. The layout also seemed a little bit different too, which prompted me to start reading all of the headlines and suggested topic areas of interest.

My eyes grew larger as I scanned the page and saw very explicit search descriptions for body parts and sexual positions that I had never heard of. *What the . . . ?* If these were my husband's searches he would definitely be smart enough to not leave them up for me to see. I quickly ruled him out. That left only one person.

I reset the home page to my standard Yahoo screen. Obviously, having the computer in my room wasn't enough. New measures to lock it down would have to be researched so that this wouldn't happen again, but for now that investigation would have to wait.

Returning to the main level of our home, I found Ella at the kitchen table coloring. I really had no idea how I was going to address this. Taking a deep breath, I dove in.

"Ella, were you using Mommy's computer?"

"Yes," Ella said tentatively. Her eyes did not leave the princess she was coloring.

Stressed, all I came up with was, "What did you do?"

"I. Don't. Know." Her voice began to quiver and she wouldn't lift her head to look at me.

Another deep breath. "Ella, were you on the Internet?"

In not much more than a whisper: "Yes." Still no eye contact.

"Ella, were you and Suzy searching for something?"

Her brown eyes finally looked up into mine. She was scared. What on earth had she seen? What had Suzy seen and how was I going to explain this to her mother?

"We were looking for . . . boobs."

Boobs. Really? Thinking back to what was on that purple search screen, I was somewhat amazed by what comes up when someone searches for "boobs." My amazement intermingled with relief at the innocence of Ella's curiosity. Okay, so there was no need to *totally* freak out.

Now I really wanted to know, why on earth was she searching for boobs on the Internet?

Ella paused and then continued. "We just wanted to see boobs, Mommy. We wanted to see what they look like. But then it came to this purple screen and we turned it off."

I got it. She wasn't a thirteen-year-old kid looking for porn, but a seven-year-old girl who realized that she would have breasts someday and wanted to know what different kinds looked like. Kids are going to be curious about what the adult body looks like. And I guess that, in one way, the Internet is to this generation as *National Geographic* magazine was to mine. It's a way to satisfy natural curiosities. The only problem is that the Internet is a lot less controlled and a lot more risqué—not to mention dangerous.

My voice softened. I wanted her to know that it was all right and perfectly normal to be curious. "Okay, honey, I understand, but you have to be careful with the computer because you never know what your search words are going to bring back. Let me see if I can find some breasts." As soon as the words escaped my mouth I thought I was going to start laughing but opted instead for a reassuring smile.

A satisfied breath filled my lungs. I was hit with something a bit odd, and I didn't lose my composure. This was truly an accomplishment considering my puritan upbringing. When I was growing up, sexuality and even the basic fundamentals of sex were simply not discussed. Questions along these lines were brusquely deflected and not addressed, as if we were perverse for the mere act of inquiring. As a growing girl I stopped asking my parents and instead received a less than ideal education from friends instead. I didn't want my daughter to repeat my experience.

"Ella, why don't you color for a little bit and Mommy will see if she can find some different pictures of breasts for you to look at, because they come in different shapes and sizes. And none are better than others, okay?" I added the last bit to begin a small lesson in personal values.

Ella looked up at me again and smiled. "Thanks, Mom."

She bowed her head over her picture and continued to color. In that moment I wanted to keep her that age and innocent for as long as possible.

Although I was concerned about what she had seen, I felt I had overcome the biggest challenge by educating her that all different types of breasts were beautiful. Using the vastness of the Internet, I figured I'd easily be able find some images to support this lesson.

I was wrong.

Initial searches of the Internet resulted in very few breasts that weren't either pornographic or an example of a medical malady. The only *normal* breasts I found were in paintings or on health sites. The medical-site breasts presented their own issues because the images of the normal breasts were often depicted as a "before" shot, next to the augmentation or "after" photograph. I didn't want to show her these out of fear that it would send the message that normal breasts aren't good enough.

At the gym I regularly see many different types of women, with body shapes and breasts of all different sizes. This is reality, not what is on the Internet, on television, or in most magazines.

Raising a daughter, I am all too aware of the risks out there— the distorted body image that is everywhere. Although it existed when I was a young girl, now it seemed like it had been taken to new levels, with women and even teens opting for aggressive forms of plastic surgery as they strive to seek physical perfection. Plastic surgery and airbrushing have created a mythical version of what a woman should look like, not what most really looked like. The result is an unrealistic standard for the average girl. Despite this new version of normal, I wanted Ella to realize that she was beautiful. I wanted her to grow up accepting herself and her body—at least the best that she could.

The search for healthy breasts, free from augmentation, was long and didn't yield much. Ultimately I had to resort to paintings and only a few photos.

With my stack of breasts in hand, I spread them out on the table before Ella and me.

Waving my hand over the pictures I said, "We women come in different sizes and colors, just like these pictures. Some of us have small breasts and others have larger breasts. Some of us have wider hips than others. But what do you think is common to all of us?"

Ella looked at me, unsure of what to say. "We're all girls?"

"Yes, we're all girls. But what else do you see?"

Studying the pictures, Ella replied, "They're different but all the same too."

"Do you think any of these women is better than the others? Are any of their bodies more beautiful than the others?"

Surveying the pictures, trying to discern an answer to my question, Ella sat there. I interrupted her silence and pointed to one image. "I think that this woman is beautiful."

Ella looked at the picture I was referring to and then at me. Then I pointed to another one and said, "I also think this woman is beautiful." I continued pointing to each of the pictures in front of us, repeating the same phrase, "This woman is beautiful," until I had repeated the phrase about all of the women.

When I was finished, Ella waved her hand over the table full of pictures and said, "They're all beautiful, right?"

"Yes, Ella, they are. Every one of these women is beautiful. Beauty comes in many forms."

We then went on to talk about her and her female friends. I drew a parallel between them and the group of women on the table. I tried to reinforce to her that there was no singular standard for beauty that she or her friends needed to conform to. Only time will tell if my message made a difference.

You can't completely protect your kids from messages of sexuality and perfect body image. They are everywhere. You can only do your best to direct them to healthy body images and do all you can to strengthen and support their self-esteem.

Allergy Mom

*Andrea's Missing Pages: When danger
really is everywhere*

IT HAD BEEN A FEW WEEKS since my husband, Stan, and I had brought Xander home. Our daughter, Audrey, was about two years old. Given that Xander was our second child, on some level I thought I had the baby thing down. I had successfully breast-fed Audrey and she didn't have any real issues. Aside from being active, even as a baby she was an easy child, and I erroneously thought my experience with Xander would be the same.

Xander, like many children, had reflux to the point that I thought it might be gastroesophageal reflux disease. While I was worried about that, I was more concerned about the severe eczema he had. It was like a diaper rash that never went away. The rash was further aggravated by Xander's seemingly contin-uous pooping, which often left his skin raw from continuous exposure. He also developed oozing sores, weeping eczema, on his face and behind his ears. To keep Xander from scratching the sores and making them worse, we had to keep socks on his hands.

There was no explanation for why my son was suffering the way he was. At that time I knew only a little bit about food allergies and allergies in general. I was aware that I shouldn't eat peanuts when I was pregnant, and so I didn't—with either of my pregnancies. Then there was my husband, who couldn't eat peanuts or strawberries, but those issues weren't as dire. Allergies, such as those to cats or bees, also ran in our family. With this basic knowledge, I began to wonder whether Xander was having an allergic reaction.

Sometimes food consumed while breast-feeding can trigger issues with babies. Was there something I could eliminate that might reduce Xander's eczema? Although I didn't experience anything similar to this when I nursed Audrey, she did develop a mild aversion to dairy—breaking out into hives at ten months old after consuming yogurt. Thinking there might be a correlation between her issue and Xander's, I gave up consuming dairy to eliminate it from my breast milk. The problem persisted. So off to the doctor we went.

"Andrea, are you eating soy?" the doctor said.

Images of all the soy lattes my thoughtful friends had been bringing me floated through my mind. As if he could see them too, the doctor responded before I could. "Maybe you should give up soy."

Willing to do whatever I possibly could for my child, I responded, "Done."

Off dairy and soy, I sought out other foods, because, well . . . I like to eat. I became a friend of simple carbohydrates and ate pasta, pretzels, and other snacks. Unfortunately all of my efforts appeared fruitless; Xander's sandpaper skin persisted.

Back to the doctor we went.

"Doc, what *is* going on?"

The doctor studied me for a moment and then responded, "Well—I hate to say it, but have you thought about giving up *wheat*?"

"Are you kidding me? Really?" I couldn't believe it. Standing in that tiny, sterile room, I flashed back to our house and could smell the gingerbread we had baked that morning. This was *not* going to be easy.

"Are you sure this is the issue?" Then in a moment of clarity, I thought to ask the next dreaded question—if for no other reason than I hated to see my son suffer. Bracing myself, I asked, "Is there anything *else*?"

"Ummm, well . . ." He paused, looking as if he were unsure how to break the rest of the news to me. "You might want to eliminate wheat . . . *and eggs*."

I was in shock. No wheat. No eggs. No dairy. No soy. What on earth would I eat? Did I mention I *like* to eat?

Determined to do whatever was needed to ease Xander's discomfort, I did as the doctor suggested. Only thirty-six hours after I eliminated all these foods from my diet, my son's skin was *clear* and the poop factory began to stabilize as well.

For now, I had won the allergy battle and Xander was at peace.

When Xander turned five months old, we decided to have him allergy tested. Opinions vary as to when testing is most effective, because babies are still developing, but given Xander's history we wanted to be proactive in determining any other potential allergens. As I expected, he tested positive for many things, including fish. Knowing that sometimes the tests aren't accurate and the actual reaction to consumption was, I would occasionally experiment and eat things to see how he would tolerate the small amounts coming through my breast milk.

By the time Xander was ten months old, I figured I had the allergy thing down. Xander couldn't consume certain things either directly or via my breast milk, but I could feed Audrey some of them. When I fed Audrey anything that might result in an allergic reaction in Xander, I would isolate her and the questionable foods while she ate them. The process was down and working well—until that one time when it didn't.

It was midweek around lunchtime. Xander was ten months old and Audrey was just under three. We had spent the morning at the house; we were going to eat lunch and then head out for a play date. I looked over to Audrey sitting at the table, happily devouring the fish sticks I had put in front of her. Xander was scooting around, safely away from where I had placed Audrey. A sense of accomplishment poured through me; this allergy thing was manageable as long as I was careful.

I turned slightly to finish packing the diaper bag for impending outdoor adventures. As I was taking inventory I heard it. Vomiting. Xander was vomiting.

Dropping everything, I saw him emerge from under where Audrey was sitting—an area littered by small particles of food dropped from her plate—his dark pants spotted by bits of tan breading and white flaky fish. As I hurried over to move him away, he stopped, turned, and vomited again.

Grabbing him, I rushed out of the room. His tiny body erupted into hives. In less than ten minutes, I removed his con-taminated clothing and bathed him—eliminating all elements of any food he might have come in contact with. Coming back into the kitchen, my heart rate began to return to normal. I buckled Xander safely in a chair and mopped up the remaining mess.

Crisis had been averted, or so I thought until I looked over to him.

As he sat in the chair, his limbs poured over the edges, his head back against the rear. He was gazing out the window and appeared on the verge of falling asleep. It was almost one o'clock, not quite his naptime, but the timing, in combination with his recent vomiting episode, might explain his listlessness. I was concerned, but not too worried.

Hoping he would sleep in the car on the way to the play date, I pulled Xander out of the chair and up over my shoulder and shepherded Audrey to the door. I made a mental note: I would definitely have to call the doctor about his strange and unusually intense reaction.

As I put Xander into his car seat and tightened the straps, I looked into his eyes. He was just looking at me—his stare distant, unlike anything I had seen before.

Nervous energy shot through me. Something was wrong. He was still having some sort of reaction. How did I miss this? I reached into his diaper bag to pull out the ever-ready bottle of allergy medicine and braced myself for his inevitable screams; he hated oral medicines.

Lifting the dropper up, I looked at him again and realized something was *really* wrong.

Xander was silent, his eyes glassy.

Panic exploded in my chest. His airways were closing!

I shot what I could of the Zyrtec into Xander's throat, pulled him out of the car seat, and dashed frantically for the house. My bewildered daughter trailed behind me.

Grabbing the kitchen phone, I dialed 911 and began infant CPR right there on the floor. I knew that if I stopped, Xander would die.

It seemed like an eternity, but he started to breathe on his own right as the fire trucks and ambulance pulled up. As the paramedics took over, I stepped back and allowed the shaking in my arms and legs to slowly subside.

And just like that, he seemed to return to normal. The antihistamine had worked.

Assured that Xander was temporarily stabilized, the paramedic said, "Ma'am, do you want us to transport your son to the ER for further evaluation?"

Dazed, but relieved, I looked at my son. He was alert and looking around. Our pediatrician had been through so much with us and knew him and his issues in detail, so I declined. "No, that's okay, I will call his pediatrician's office instead."

I now know that was the absolute wrong thing to do. What I didn't know then was that a person can have a second-wave reaction anywhere from four to seven hours after the initial attack. Xander should have been transported in an ambulance with an EpiPen.

Luckily we didn't have any more episodes that day, but what I soon realized was that no matter what I do, my son can never truly be safe. As an allergy mom, I have to be prepared for everything—from a minor reaction to a life-threatening one. I can't just hop in the car and go out. I never travel anywhere without wipes, an antihistamine, and at least four EpiPens. We can't simply go to a birthday party—we have to pack our own food. He is young enough now that he doesn't fully grasp the social impact, but I know in time he will.

The strange thing about allergies is that they can appear at any time. They can be triggered by something in the air, from innocent contact, or through ingestion. Every day brings with it one big question mark. As a parent I want someone to tell me exactly what I have to worry about and take on to protect my child. Just tell me because I'll do it. But no one can tell you because it is a dynamic issue. It is the not knowing that's the worst. As a result, I take one day at a time . . . hoping I never again have to witness my son on the thin edge between life and death.

Some of us didn't expect that when we became parents, life would be this intense—that our children would need so much protection just to exist. Life likes to throw curve balls, and it is in the face of these unknown challenges resulting in dynamic situations that we have to navigate ways to provide healthy and supportive environments for our children. If you have a child with allergies or other special needs, educate yourself and seek out communities of parents with like issues. If you don't have a child with these issues, try to educate yourself on what your child's peer is going through because your awareness and understanding can go far in easing the dangers in that kid's life.
For those seeking information or support for a child with allergies, below are some helpful websites:

www.foodallergy.org

www.kidswithfoodallergies.org

A Teenage Romance
for the Ages

Liesl's Missing Pages: When your teenager lies

CAREFUL NOT TO SLIP on an intermittent patch of ice, I pulled my hat down farther over my ears. As much as I was enjoying this time with my sister, I was certainly not enjoying the Pittsburgh winter wonderland. These walks gave us time to enjoy the fresh—okay, ridiculously cold—air and to discuss our kids. Right now my other three children, a boy and girl in elementary school and another girl in middle school, seemed to be stable, despite the recent separation from their father. Julie, my sixteen-year-old child from a previous relationship, on the other hand, was another story. It seemed that Julie was testing new boundaries with wild haircuts and unauthorized piercings, among a host of things.

What troubled me most was that she had suddenly become intensely involved with a new boyfriend, Jay. Although I had met his family, I knew very little about him, and the intensity of her focus was concerning.

On the surface, Jay seemed like a good enough kid. He lived at home and had a job. But he also seemed . . . directionless. Recently out of high school, he said he wasn't ready for college yet, but he also had no idea what he wanted to do with his life. Then there were the other troubling signs, like the underage drinking that I had recently found out about. I was a teenager once too, but it seemed like the excessive drinking was starting earlier than it did when I was younger.

"This is screwed up," I said to my sister. "This teenage kid is working at JRoss and his boss is giving him drinks. I mean, come on, he's underage and—"

"Liesl," my sister interrupted, awkwardly, "I . . . I don't think he's underage."

Abruptly I stopped and turned to her. "What?" I pictured Jay in my mind and he looked *really* young. "What do you mean, he's not underage?"

My sister shifted her weight; averting her eyes from mine, she studied the pavement beneath our feet. Finally looking back at me, she said, "Well . . . I didn't know how to tell you this, because Julie told Jackie in confidence, but . . . he's twenty-five."

Instantly, anger swelled up inside me. It must have been apparent to my sister, because she quickly added, "But maybe Julie's making it up. I mean, maybe she's just trying to impress her cousin."

Our walk was cut short right after that comment. I had work to do before my kids came home from school.

After returning to the house, I didn't bother taking off my coat before going on the Internet—it really is amazing what you can find with Google. A simple search yielded a link to Jay's MySpace page, which conveniently enough listed his birthday; he was indeed twenty-five.

Staring at his picture, I wondered, *Is he a sexual predator?* Vague recollections of stories that he had dated a woman several years his senior floated up. Maybe he wasn't a predator, but I really didn't know what to believe anymore. It was time to call my attorney and assess my options.

Placing the phone back in the cradle, I caught sight of the image of Julie on my desk. At sixteen, she was striking. Although not a classic Hollywood beauty, she had an amazing figure—one that caused many heads to turn when we were out. I had witnessed older men look at her twice, obviously thinking she was older than her actual age. Maybe that was what attracted Jay to her—I really didn't know—but at only sixteen this couldn't continue.

The next call I made was one I will not soon forget. Thankfully I had Jay's home number from the countless evenings Julie had spent there.

"Hey, Kim, how are you? It's Liesl, Julie's mother."

Kim, Jay's mother, seemed a little surprised by my call, given that we had met only once briefly, but she was friendly all the same.

"I'm good, Liesl. What can I do for you?"

Deep breath.

"I was wondering: how old do you think Julie is?"

Silence.

Then Kim said, "Eighteen."

"That's funny," I responded, "I thought Jay was eighteen!"

Silence.

"Oh no. . . . How old *is* Julie?"

"She's only sixteen," I replied.

Kim drew a sharp breath. "Oh, *no!*"

"Oh yes, Kim. Listen, I really care about Jay and wish him a lot of luck. But I don't want them to have contact. This is where it ends. Period." As expected, there was no resistance from Kim; now I just needed to wait for Julie to get home from school. I had only a little time to speak to her privately before the younger children came home on the bus.

When Julie arrived at the house, I called out to her from the kitchen. Entering it, she grabbed a bottle of water and plopped into the wooden chair at the kitchen table where I was already seated.

"Julie. I understand that you are in love." Julie rolled her eyes. Already my words were being discounted. She had no idea what I was about to say next.

"And had you been honest with me about Jay's age, then you wouldn't have the heartbreak that you are about to experience, because I would've had you end this relationship long before it got this far and you became this involved with him."

Julie's eyes filled with tears and her shoulders sagged. "But Mom, I *love* him."

"Well, if you really love this boy as much as you claim, then you'd realize that he's beautiful and would make some lonely prisoner an awesome cellmate. It ends now, Julie. You will be grounded for the next few weeks for not being honest with me."

Julie dragged her feet along the wooden floor, sullenly retreating up the stairs to her room. She was heartbroken, but overall it went better than expected. I truly didn't think it was going to be this easy.

Several weeks past and there was nothing. No indication of any contact with Jay. The troubled storm appeared to have passed, and Julie was finally earning her freedom back. Bit by bit, I began to trust her again. Her first night out since being grounded would be spent with Corinna, a close friend whom I knew very well. With her out, and the other children with their father for the weekend, I was looking forward to having an evening of peace and quiet. Unfortunately things don't always go as planned.

That night, a few hours after she left, I found myself pacing back and forth. Something wasn't right. I couldn't call her, because I had taken her cell phone away—after she had accumulated $1,600 in cell phone charges over three short months. Fortunately, I did have most of her friends' numbers in my cell phone—including Corinna's. Maybe I was overreacting, but after her previous lying regarding Jay's age and my unsettled feeling, I wanted to verify that she was really at Corinna's house.

I sent a text: *Please have Julie call me.*

Within minutes, Corinna's phone number popped up on my Caller ID. It was Julie. We talked briefly and I hung up.

Time passed, but the nagging sensation did not. I texted Corinna again to have Julie call me. Within minutes, Corinna's number popped up and Julie was on the line. We spoke briefly and I hung up. I probably should have been reassured, but wasn't.

Shortly after our call, my cell phone rang and it was Amelia, one of Julie's friends.

"Hey, Mrs. Hoffman, is Julie there?"

With tempered confidence, I replied, "She's spending the night at Corinna's."

"That's strange, I just called there and she wasn't there. I guess I'll try again."

My unease was founded. "That *is* strange, Amelia. Thanks for calling."

I texted Corinna again and asked once more for Julie to call me.

The phone rang, complete with Corinna's number.

"Hey, Jules, what's going on?"

"Uhh, yeah, Mom. I was in the shower and Corinna was lying down."

"You're at Corinna's house, right?"

"Yeah."

"Great. Then I will see you in a half hour." I hung up the phone.

No sooner had I hung up than I heard my cell phone ring, and Corinna's number appeared again.

This should be interesting.

"Ahhh, Mrs. Hoffman. Julie isn't here." Corinna was scared and had every reason for being so.

"Oh, really, then where is she?"

"Umm. I think she is with Amelia . . . somewhere." The strain in Corinna's voice spoke louder than the words she uttered.

"That's funny, because Amelia called me looking for her."

Dead silence.

"Before I go further, I'd like to know how it is she is calling me from a separate location, but your number is coming up."

At this point Corinna figured out that she ought to start coming clean. "I . . . um . . . have three-way calling. I call her and call you and then my number comes up on your phone."

"Listen, Corinna, you obviously know how to get hold of her. I want you to call her and have her call me directly from the phone that she is really on."

Hanging up the phone, I knew where I was going to look next. As a parent you often hope for the best but are always pre-pared for the worst.

Scrolling through the names, I came to Jay's. I texted Jay: *Is Julie with you?*

His text response was a quick denial: *No, Mrs. Hoffman. I'm at a concert over an hour away in Ohio. I haven't seen Julie. I wouldn't go near her, not with the threat of jail.*

He was undoubtedly lying, but it was Julie's repeated lies that ate at me. I didn't respond back.

I sat there waiting on the sofa near the large picture win-dow. The window held little except a dark winter night, and somewhere within it my daughter. The chirp of my cell phone disrupted my thoughts. It was her.

"Julie, where are you?"

"Ohio."

Here we go, I thought. *Let's see how far she will take this.*

"Have you seen Jay?"

I could only imagine the shock and concern on her face. *Yes, little girl, you are completely busted.*

"No. Um, I mean, he's here at this concert, but I haven't seen him."

The anger swelled within me. I was a teenager once, too, of course . . . and actually quite the wild child in my own right. I had been there. I had seen and done a lot of things when I was younger. I broke rules and made a lot of mistakes. Each time my parents were there to discipline me, or pick me up and guide me back to where I needed to be. I may not have liked their methods, but still, my parents did their job. Now I needed to do mine, as Julie's mother.

"Do you think I'm a complete idiot?" I said.

"No, Mom . . . I don't," she said in a quieter voice.

"Then get your butt home."

I pressed the End button on my phone and stared at it. Anger boiled within me. I was furious about her lies and deception, and angry with myself for not catching things sooner and preventing this. As I paced back and forth I weighed my next move. It was already very late, and I knew that if I tried to talk to her that moment it would be ugly and I would say something that I might regret and cause irreparable damage.

As certain as I had been that something was wrong, I was equally certain it would be better to wait until morning before I fully addressed this.

We lived in a small Cape Cod–style home, where I occupied a bedroom on the main level toward the front of the house. My room allowed me visibility into the street, which was often handy in monitoring Julie's comings and goings. It was late and it would take her a few hours to make it home from Ohio; it made sense to get ready for bed and lie there waiting for her.

The headlights turning into the driveway reflected off my

dresser mirror, breaking the darkness and alerting me to her arrival. The creak of the door and subsequent unlatching, followed by Julie's footsteps on the wooden floors, let me know that she was inside.

Chilled, I wrapped my robe around my waist and left my room, headed for the living room where I knew she would be. I flicked the light switch on, causing Julie to jump slightly. She turned to look at me and then averted her eyes, instead focusing on the sleeves of her coat.

Silence filled the room as I stood there with my arms crossed, looking at her.

Julie broke the quiet. "Mom . . ." she began, with her arms outstretched and her head tilted, now looking at me, prepared to plead with me.

I held my hand up to stop her from saying anything more and calmly said, "*Don't*, Julie. Go to bed. We'll speak about this in the morning." Then, cinching my robe a little tighter, I turned and walked away.

Julie stood there, her eyes wide and mouth agape, not sure what to make of our interaction. She mumbled, "Okay," and retreated to the safety of her bedroom.

Once in bed, I couldn't sleep; my mind refused to be muted.

I had Julie when I was young and basically raised her alone because her father had been largely absent from her life. Every time he forgot her birthday or didn't follow through on something, we discussed it. I always felt it was better to discuss the real man rather that the prince who doesn't exist.

Later, when I married Phil and we had our three children, I thought he would be a good male figure in Julie's life. For many years things went well—that is, until Phil had an affair and our marriage crumbled. Raising children is difficult enough, let alone when you do it on your own. I never thought I would be in this lonely, difficult place. Maybe Julie had been impacted more than I thought from all of this, or maybe it was merely teenage rebellion. Regardless, the lying seemed to be forming a pattern and it needed to stop.

I got up before Julie, went to the kitchen, and was making coffee when she came downstairs. I sensed her presence behind me and said, "Before we talk about anything, you do know that you're once again grounded. This time I don't have any idea when it will end because it needs to address two issues. First, you went to a concert, in another state, with Jay, all of which is forbidden. Second, you lied to me and went so far as to involve your friends in your web of lies." I turned around, and my eyes met hers. "You know you hurt me."

"Yeah, I know, Mom." Julie looked down as if studying the edge of the kitchen table.

Did she really know? Did she understand that the only way I could look out for her, help her in her life outside this house, was for her to be honest with me? At sixteen I doubted it, but at minimum she needed to know how deeply her deception had hurt me.

"I give my love to you kids freely. Trust is initially given, but once it's broken, it needs to be earned back. Each time you lie to me, it breaks that trust further until I no longer believe anything that you say. The only way to get back that trust, that bond with me, is to build it slowly. You need to give me reasons, to show me, that I can have faith that you are telling me the truth."

My words hung in the air a moment. Then I added, "Julie, I love you. But, you must know that I don't trust you, that our bond has a crack in it right now."

"I know." My daughter's large brown eyes left the table and met mine, in them an acknowledgment of her actions and her uncertainty regarding the future and our relationship.

"All right," I said, "we'll just have to work our way back to each other from here."

No matter how close you are to your teenager, they are probably not always going to be honest with you. Trust, but verify what you are told. If the lying becomes a pattern, then you need to discuss it with them and explain how their lies have hurt or impacted you or others. If your teenager is caught in a lie, there should be a punishment for the action and for the lie. Having consequences for both reinforces the fact that lying is not acceptable.

That's Not a Toilet!

Terry's Missing Pages: When your child goes to the bathroom in an unexpected location

THROWING THE LAST of the sandwich crusts and mangled orange pieces into the trash, I stopped for a moment to sit at the edge of the baby pool. This was one of those days when I felt that I had it together. The swimming lessons had gone off without a tantrum, we were on time for our picnic lunch at the pool, and now we had time for a little postlunch play before we'd have to leave to get home for the kids' naps. Yup, I had this mom thing under control.

Full from lunch and warmed from the sun, I leaned back and watched my kids play, relishing their giggles. My daughter, Isabelle, who was a little over a year old, splashed her arms, at times appearing genuinely startled when the water landed in her face. Then there was my three-year-old son, Max, who was running circles around her, pretending he was a train—complete with sound effects. It was perfection, until I noticed that Max had stopped running.

Max abruptly stopped and stood in the middle of the pool, with one hand over his groin and the other over his rear.

"Mommy, I gotta go nowwwwwww!"

As any parent with small children knows, when you see a child trying to control himself by placing his hands over the insistent areas, you have approximately two seconds before all hell breaks loose and you have a disaster on your hands.

I waded over and swooped both Max and Isabelle out of the pool. With Isabelle cradled on my hip and my other hand on Max's shoulder, I steered him out of the gated confines of the baby pool and toward the bathhouse.

"Mommmm, I wanna go into the boys' room."

We were now T minus one second from disaster.

Peering my head around the corner, I hollered into the men's room. "Hellooooo. Anyone in there?" A few seconds passed: nothing but silence.

Grateful the bathroom was empty, I nudged Max into the room. "Go, honey. Mommy will stand right here. If anyone comes in, don't talk to them. Just go."

Max disappeared into the men's room.

With no flushing or obvious hand washing Max reappeared a few moments later. *This is not good*, I thought.

"Mommy, I can't find where to flush the potty. I can't flush number two."

Well, that at least explained why I hadn't heard a toilet flush. Once again I hollered into the bathroom. Assured it was empty, I walked in.

"Max, baby, where is this potty?"

My eyes followed to where his little arm was pointing, and slowly I pieced together why the potty didn't flush. It was a urinal!

Holy crap! I mean really, CRAP!

I walked over to the urinal, and it sank in that my son had just *sat in a urinal*!

EWWWWWWW!

Disgust mixed with panic rose within me.

I surveyed the small room. There were no paper towels to be found. No way to remedy this. Since I couldn't easily resolve the issue, I shifted to the more immediate concern, which was that my three-year-old needed to be brought home and bathed. I took Max over to the sink, where we washed our hands, then walked over to the pool to retrieve the stroller, which was still packed to the gills with a colorful array of pool toys and floats.

Approaching the lifeguards, I quickly debated what, if anything, I should say. Knowing that it really needed to be addressed, but not wanting to be too obvious with our rapid departure, I casually said, "Uh, there is a mess in the men's bathroom you might want to clean up."

Mortified, I walked home with my two children. I would probably forever be known as the mom whose kid mistook the urinal for a toilet. So much for my perfect, well-planned day. At that moment I recognized I had a choice to make: I could either continue to be upset and embarrassed, or I could laugh and accept it for what it was. The words of wisdom that I had received at Max's baby shower filled my head: "If you think you will laugh about it someday, you ought to just start laughing, because parenthood is full of surprises."

I spent the next block and a half laughing.

Life sometimes hands you the unexpected. If you are going to laugh about it someday, you might as well start now.

Living with a
Train Wreck Every Day

*Sally's Missing Pages: When your child has
substance abuse issues*

I DON'T KNOW WHAT HAPPENED with my boys. All of them
experimented with drugs—in differing degrees. While the two
girls excelled at school and were generally well behaved, the
three boys put us through many years of the Richmond police
coming to our door. My husband, Greg, and I went to "tough
love" classes, read books, and attended programs. Eventually the
older two boys came out of it after a few years. Dillon didn't.

Dillon is now thirty and has spent half of his life as an
addict; his addiction is a tsunami that sweeps into his life and the
lives of those around him and then sucks him away deeper and
deeper, leaving nothing but destruction in its aftermath. Dillon
has missed birthdays, births of nieces and nephews, funerals,

and weddings—either because he was in jail or because he was so high he might as well not have been there. I often wonder, how can he want a life like that? I know it's not that he *wants* it—but by failing to admit he has a problem and getting clean, he has time and again made his choice.

And yet we still keep hoping. Perhaps it's because we have seen the other two come around, battle their issues, and integrate into normal society. At other times I think it's what every parent of an addict hopes for—that one day their child will hit "rock bottom," wake up, realize the damage he has done, and become committed to being clean. As a mother of an addict, I continually struggle between loving my son and at the same time not supporting his choices for his life.

A year ago Dillon moved back home and seemed sincere about truly being clean and sober. He was recently released after his most recent stint in a Virginia jail, but he seemed happy— more content than I had ever seen him. Before he was incarcerated, he had met a girl from North Carolina and appeared to really be in love.

Right after he moved back home, we sat down and gave him the house rules. To get to a point where he could live on his own, he would need to rebuild his life—one step at a time. He would need to work, to reestablish his credit and credibility. Because we loved our son and wanted to support what we saw as positive life changes, we helped him. We lent him a car and advised him on how to reestablish a bank account and a credit card with a $500 limit on it. Everything was held jointly with him so we could monitor it and catch any red flags.

Dillon began to work and slipped nicely back into the family. I remember at times looking at him, amazed at how *clear* he looked. He was clearer than I ever remembered having seen him. Then within a few months the problems began.

It was nothing major at first, but then I noticed there was a lot of money flowing through his account. There would be times when his account was full and then the next day virtually empty. Checks were bouncing. Because the limited credibility he had built was broken, we assumed control over the accounts. At the same time, he moved out and into a house with friends.

From that point on he was aloof, only sporadically attending family functions. Each time he was distant, but still significantly better than he had been before his stint in jail. A small strand of hope remained.

One night he sat us down and told us of his plans to move to North Carolina with his girlfriend, Bryn, to get a new start. Maybe he needed a move, to be completely away from all that reminded him of his old ways and triggers. Often that is what addicts need to help break them of their cycles, their patterns of behavior. We were cautiously optimistic for his future.

The night before Dillon left, we threw a good-bye party for Bryn and him. Friends and family gathered; the warmth was palpable. Seeing Dillon and Bryn together smiling and laughing brought me happiness. I was elated that Dillon was starting over and had found someone to love.

As I was winding up work on the afternoon of their departure, the phone rang.

"When are you coming home?" Greg asked, his tone firm, noncommittal. After nearly forty years of marriage, I knew that the *only* time Greg called to ask when I was coming home was to tell me bad news. I left immediately.

Walking into the house, I heard the sound of running water from the kitchen. Entering it I found Greg doing dishes. Seeing me, he turned off the water, dried his hands and leaned against the sink. "Sally, I need you to sit down."

The gravity on Greg's face spoke volumes. I reached a kitchen chair and readied myself for what was to come.

"Dillon has been arrested again."

I checked my watch; I couldn't believe what I was hearing. He left only six hours ago! Disbelief gave way to anger—the cycle had begun yet again. Once more we had supported him, loved him, and tried to help him build a new life, and again he had thrown it all away. My body tensed, filled with emotion, a sharp contrast to the warmth and joy present just a few hours ago when I had seen them off. At moments like these, I had a hard time reconciling my emotions. How can you have such intense, conflicting feelings toward one person all at the same time?

"What the heck happened?" My voice edged higher than it probably should have.

"Bryn was driving and got pulled over for speeding. You'd think that being from the Carolinas she would know not to speed there. Well, she did, and then they ran the tags on his car. There were two warrants out for his arrest—one for Virginia and the other for North Carolina."

"Are you kidding me? One for Virginia? He just left here! What the heck was it for?"

Greg was pale, his face visibly tired from years of events much like this one. Crossing the room, he settled into the chair across from me at the table. He leaned forward on his elbows, placed his head in his hands and took a deep breath before speaking further.

"Apparently his probation was not finished in Virginia, like he told us. And in North Carolina, they have a warrant for theft—they have pictures of him using another person's credit card. All I can think is that he did that offense prior to his last round in jail, and it's just now catching up to him." Greg looked away from me and didn't say anything more. My heart broke. The last time this happened, it nearly destroyed my husband. Greg blamed himself and often asked me where he had gone wrong as a parent. The look on his face told me that he was blaming himself all over again. Greg was unable to separate his emotions—love for his son and feeling responsible for the choices Dillon made.

"Where's Bryn?"

"She's at a hotel. It was late when this all finished, and she said she was going to stay there before driving any farther. I think she's really shaken."

"She's not the only one," I responded.

Once again Dillon had upended his life and, to a certain extent, ours. But I didn't have time to think about that; I needed to feed our family dinner.

Setting out the dishes, I heard the phone ring.

"Sally speaking," I answered.

"Mrs. Cahill?"

"Bryn?"

"Yes—I didn't know who else to call. After they took Dillon, I was very upset and I didn't feel I was safe to drive. So I came to a hotel and simply had to know."

"Had to know what, Bryn?"

It was as if the other end of the phone had died, but I heard Bryn's breathing and gentle sobbing. Then she spoke. "If he was using again, Mrs. Cahill."

I knew what was coming. Realization washed over me. How could I have been this blind? The signs had been there. The money disappearing. Dillon moving out. I knew he'd moved out because I would have seen more, would have called him on it if he were still here. In my heart I knew, but once again I didn't want to believe—as a mother I wanted infinitely more for him.

She continued. "I went through his bags and I found pot and meth."

Geez, Dillon. Cocaine was bad . . . but meth? "I'm sorry, Bryn. We'll make arrangements for the car, but use it until then."

I heard her crying on the other end of the phone, and then she said, "I thought he loved me. I thought he had changed."

How many times had I felt her pain, had our family felt that pain—the pain of living each day watching a train wreck over and over again, but being powerless to stop it?

"Bryn, you need to listen to me. This is his choice and to a certain extent his biology. He is an addict. He will always be one; his brain will always respond in the same way to these substances until he makes a choice to accept that he has a problem and really embrace rehabilitation and the lifelong commitment that comes with it. Until he does those things, he will not change." She continued to cry on the other end. "I know you're thinking, 'If I love him enough he will want to change.' But a drug addict can only choose to change because he wants it for himself."

Completely drained, I hung up. Once again we would bear witness to the aftermath of Dillon's addiction—the conflicting emotions of love and anger battling within us. As parents we are innately programmed to love, care for, and protect our children. This becomes complicated when you're the parent of an addict because you can't protect them from their disease, or the choices they make because of it.

When events like these happen, when Dillon's addiction seeps back into our lives, I know I need to give myself time to regroup, not only for me and but also for my family.

The day following Dillon's departure and the news of his arrest, I sat down in our sunroom with my journal. Staring out at the backyard I could almost see the image of Dillon as a young and innocent boy running around with his brothers. In that moment I allowed myself to grieve for my son—to feel anger toward the addiction that once again controlled his life.

Opening my journal to the most recent entry, which followed Dillon's last arrest and incarceration, I came back to the words I had written at the bottom of it: *You Must Detach.*

Detaching with love is a principle I learned through meetings that I had attended. Detachment doesn't mean I stop loving or caring for my son. Instead, I focus on accepting that I can't change what is beyond my control—namely, Dillon's addiction. I remind myself that he is an addict trapped in an overpowering illness. I know I can love him while not loving the disease.

Intellectually I understand the process, but it doesn't mean it's easy to separate my emotions. But for the preservation of our family, and of myself, I know we must detach from him—*I* must detach from him. It's something that takes time and continual practice, and even after all of this time, I still don't have it mastered. At this point, all I can do is continue to try.

Being a parent to an addict can be crushing.
No matter how many programs you attend, how much
tough love you dole out, or how much love you give,
only an addict can choose to change because they want it.
Detaching with love from your addicted child is one
of the many elements needed for the parents of an addict.
It means letting go of the innate need and desire to help
and protect them. Doing so will make it easier for you
to return to a more stable world. You can still love
your child, but detach from and not support their choices.
For additional resources, please visit:

www.nar-anon.org

www.casacolumbia.org

www.drugabuse.gov/publications/drugfacts/
understanding-drug-abuse-addiction

Monkey See, Monkey Do

*Ted's Missing Pages: When you didn't realize
that you were setting the wrong example*

BIT BY BIT THE COLORFUL PLASTIC pieces built upon each other.
I watched as my son deftly manipulated the small Lego pieces.
Although it was only October, it was like Christmas for my five-
year-old. I had recently unearthed my box of childhood Lego
blocks. He had mixed them with his own and was now actively
engaged in creating a masterpiece.

I heard the sound of small pieces being taken apart and
looked beyond the Sunday paper to see what the issue was. Then
I saw that familiar look: the red frustration creeping up his neck
and into his face. It was the look of impending meltdown.

"Dude. What's wrong?"

"It's not right, Dad! It's just not right." Anger crept into his
voice. "This is horrible. I can't do anything right."

"That's not true." Putting the paper down, I sat on the floor next to him.

Keith's big brown eyes were brimming with tears. The pain of his perceived failure spread across his furrowed brow.

"Why do you think it's not right? What's wrong with it? I think it looks fantastic! Look at how well you built this wall, door and . . . what's this?" I said, pointing to the intricate wall he had built.

I hoped the diversion from the problem area would calm him and help him realize that what he had built was really quite creative. For a moment I saw him look at the wall, his tears ceasing.

"It's a storage area for the king's treasures. But it doesn't matter anyway because this tower doesn't look right and I can't make a good one." The remaining blocks tumbled from his hands and made a gentle landing on the Berber carpet. Keith sat there looking at them, unmoving.

My diversion tactics had not worked, but what puzzled me more was why Keith was incredibly hard on himself. Even if it was good, unless it was perfect by his definition, it was a failure in his eyes. From a very early age Keith had been a perfectionist, even meticulously lining his Matchbox cars up. But outwardly verbalizing his frustration with himself was new, and more extreme.

I picked up the offending Lego blocks in front of Keith and held them in my hands. I didn't want to see him give up on himself like this. Bending down slightly, so his face was visible, I said, "Hey, K-dawg, it's okay, really. I think you did a great job. I like how you used these special angled pieces at the top. Do you want me to help you? We could do it together."

"No thanks, Dad. I don't want to work on it right now. I wanted to do it by myself, but I can't get it right. I don't wanna try anymore." With that Keith stood up and walked away, leaving the partially destroyed wall unrepaired.

The intense criticism that Keith inflicted on himself was painful to watch. My wife, Liz, walked in as Keith was leaving, his eyes downcast and his hands firmly planted in his pockets. I looked to her, completely perplexed as to what to do with our child. As she put our daughter into the highchair, she said, "The apple doesn't fall far from the tree."

Standing up, I placed the blocks on the ground near the wall in hopes that maybe with a little break he might come back to his project.

"Yeah, I know I was just like him as a kid," I replied. I could identify. The similarities between us were almost spooky at times. But I knew I had grown out of it, or more realistically learned to generally control it, and hoped he would as well.

The next weekend I was repairing something in the garage. No matter what I seemed to do, it would not work correctly.

Sitting there on the cold concrete floor, I had parts spread around me, my back to the open garage door. These were new parts fresh out of the box, parts that should fit but inexplicably didn't. It was ridiculous. The irritation rose within me, tension filling my shoulders.

The door opened and my wife walked out to put groceries in our garage freezer.

Glancing toward her, I said, "I don't know why I even bother to try to fix anything around here. I clearly don't know what parts to get or else this would be done by now, and I wouldn't be wasting all this time." The parts dropped from my hands onto the concrete garage floor. I stared with dread at my project.

I felt Liz looking at me, but then I saw that she was gazing past me. Turning toward the doorway, I saw the outline of my son, Keith, partially mounted on his bike. Had he been there the whole time?

"Keith, honey, why don't you show Mommy and Daddy one more time how you can go around the cul-de-sac on your new big-boy bike?" my wife said as she grabbed my hand, pulled me up off the floor, and led me outside. In a low whisper she added, "I need to talk to you."

With the fall sun shining down on our son, we watched as he circled around and around, faster and faster. As nice as it was to stand and watch, I really didn't understand why Liz had pulled me out here when I had a project to finish.

"You wanted to talk—what's up? I need to figure out where I'm going wrong in there with the parts I just bought."

Turning toward me, she would not let go of my hand and gave it a strong squeeze. By the look it her eyes, I knew I wasn't going anywhere until she was finished.

"You know last week when I said the apple doesn't fall far from the tree?"

Pulling from her, I crossed my arms. "Yeah, why? It doesn't. He's just like I was at that age."

"No, Ted, he's just like you are right now."

Before I could say anything, she continued. "You're both perfectionists; he is mimicking your behavior. You were really hard on yourself there, just like he had been. Remember that saying, 'Monkey see, monkey do'? Well, Keith is watching us both and absorbing how we handle things. Right or wrong, he responds in a way that he thinks we would."

I took a deep breath and looked at Keith, smiling as he rode around the circle. As a child I had been just like my son and became frustrated easily with my projects or clumsy attempts at new activities. If I couldn't do it perfectly, I didn't want to do it. As an adult I learned to mostly work through those issues and had come a long way—or at least I usually applied filters to keep from saying out loud what I really wanted to express. But today I obviously hadn't used any filters, or reined in my bad attitude— and my son had witnessed all of it.

She continued, "I think we both need to continue to give

him positive reinforcement when he tries something—letting him know that it is okay to strive for perfection, but we don't expect it. Maybe we could reinforce to him that sometimes the way to get to perfection is through trying new ways and ideas—even if it might initially mean failure."

Pausing, she looked at Keith riding triumphantly up the driveway and added, "I think we both need to watch our interaction not only with each other and our kids, but also with ourselves. The reality is they pick up on everything we do—including those things that are inwardly directed."

Before he could get to the top of the driveway, Liz had released my hand and walked down to greet him. I watched as she hugged him, and then I too walked down and joined her in praising Keith's newly found bike-riding skills.

From that point forward, we both made a conscious effort to watch our self-criticism and all of our behavior.

One day, after the garage incident, I was mowing the lawn and Keith was out running around the backyard. Midway through mowing, the lawn mower started to make an awful sound. Keith cruised over toward me as I turned it off, curious as to what the problem was. Initially I thought something from the yard had flung up and jammed the blade, but further inspection revealed that wasn't the case. For the next few hours I took the lawn mower apart. Periodically Keith would make his way over to examine my progress and I would explain what I had discovered, or not discovered, was the problem. We talked about how although it bugged Daddy that he couldn't fix the problem quickly, the important thing was to move forward. That if I walked away, the mower would never get fixed. But as I kept working through the problem I was actually one step closer to figuring it out. Eventually I fixed the problem and had turned it into a great teachable moment for my son.

I didn't realize then what a positive impact the lawn mower

incident had had on Keith until a few weeks later. Keith was in the family room with our daughter, Kylie, and their cousin Cora, who were both almost two. Cora was visiting for the weekend and they were all sitting around and playing with the large Duplo blocks. I was in the adjoining kitchen preparing my lunch when I heard the clatter of the blocks falling to the ground. Then I heard Keith counseling the younger girls.

"It's okay, guys. We can fix this. Sometimes you have to try a few times to get things the way you want them."

A smile spread across my face—now this was a behavior of mine I didn't mind being mimicked.

*You are your own reality show. Like it or not, our kids
are watching our every move and response.
Monkey see, monkey do. If we don't want to see negative behaviors
in them, we need to model the behaviors we do want.*

Not Struggling, Just Bored

*Loren's Missing Pages: When your child's
school can't meet her needs*

STARING AT THE E-MAIL on my computer, I was perplexed.
Quinn had never had academic issues. For a moment I wondered
if they had her confused with another child in her second grade
class. But no, this e-mail specifically mentioned her.

Dear Mr. & Mrs. Ellis,

*I have some concerns about Quinn. Recently I've noticed that she is
having trouble with class concepts and focusing in class. Have you observed
any of this at home? I would like to meet to discuss some possible interven-
tions that could be put in place to assist her with the curriculum.*

Let me know what your schedule is so that we could set up a conference.

Regards,

Mrs. Miller

Oakwood Elementary, 2nd Grade

I found it hard to believe that Quinn was having a problem, because she always seemed to be ahead of her peers. She was articulate for her age, an early reader, math came easily—it didn't add up. But if she was having trouble, I wanted to get on top of the issue as quickly as possible. With the note in hand, I called the school and scheduled the conference.

Walking outside, I watched as Quinn and Sebastian, our aged dachshund, played in the backyard. Dressed as a fairy princess, my daughter had created an imaginary world in which they had to find the clues to discover where her fairy sister was being held captive. Quinn caught me looking at her, and her blue eyes lit up with delight. I was busted.

A broad smile spread across my face as I assumed the persona of the evil fairy queen. With a dramatic sweep of my arm, I wrapped my sweater coat around me. "You will never figure out where I've hidden her!" I leaned my head back and let out a cackling laugh. *"Haaaa haaa haa ha."*

My feigned evil laugh was overridden by the joyful giggles of Quinn, her copper curls bouncing in time with her laughter.

She seemed happy and normal, but was she also struggling? Maybe I was delusional, but I would think that if she was truly having trouble at school, I would see other signs too, that there might be emotional manifestations of the problems she was having. Quinn often gets moody when something is bugging her, but her temperament was anything but that. There were simply no emotional signs to indicate a problem.

The next morning while the children were in gym class, I sat at a miniature table, my knees barely able to slide under it, while her teacher and I went over Quinn's latest work.

"You see, Mrs. Ellis, Quinn seems incapable of completing many of her assignments. Even on tests she will forget to fill out whole pages."

There it was right in front of me in black and white—Quinn's test paper, empty except for her name and a few answers here and there.

My thoughts were interrupted. "And . . . she often just sits here looking out the window . . . She simply is not paying attention."

Hmmm. I guess neither was I. Something was definitely wrong. But what? Quinn had been having issues sleeping. Maybe we needed to talk to her pediatrician and ask for recommendations for stretches or way to mitigate the charley horses that were keeping her up at night. There had to be some rational explanation for what I was seeing.

I looked up at the teacher. "Mrs. Miller, I see what you've given me, but I've gotta say this simply doesn't make sense. Quinn did incredibly well in first grade."

"Well, I don't know what to tell you except she appears to not be focused, and her lack of focus appears to be impacting her ability to perform."

I thanked her as graciously as possible and left the room, unclear as to where to go from here.

During dinner that night, my husband, Richard, and I casually broached the subject of school.

"Soooo," I said, followed by a ridiculously long pause, "How's second grade going? Do you like it?"

"No, not really." Quinn wouldn't lift her eyes to look at us. Instead, she was intently focused on pushing her remaining bite of broccoli from one side of the plate to the other.

"Why? There's got to be *something* you like." Richard paused. "How about today? Did you learn anything new today?"

"Nope. Just same ole stuff. It's really boring."

Richard shot me a look. Clearly he was not getting anywhere and it was my turn.

"Quinn, I talked to Mrs. Miller today and she says you're

not paying attention. That you're not completing your work, your tests."

I waited to see her reaction. There wasn't one. No anxiety, no stress, nothing but an admission of guilt.

"I know. I get bored. They do the same stuff all the time. I know it. Why do I have to keep proving that I know it?"

Richard responded, "Well, that's just how things are sometimes, Quinn. They want to make sure you haven't forgotten. Even if you know it, you still have to try."

Chewing her last bite of broccoli, Quinn nodded, a small acknowledgment to us, but nothing more. She slid her dish off the table and put it in the kitchen before retreating to the living room to read.

With Quinn safely out earshot, we cleared the dishes and discussed what she had said. What if she did know the material and was simply bored? Yes, she should be completing her work, but what if her lack of motivation was because things were too easy for her?

The next day I met with the principal and discussed my concerns. We reviewed all of Quinn's first grade work, her standardized test scores, everything—and came up with nothing. No reason why she should be doing this poorly—except the possibility that she was not being challenged. He suggested having her tested, which is exactly what we did.

We were not prepared for the results.

Her IQ tested at 170. A normal score would have been around 100.

We were stunned . . . *and* delighted. It wasn't that she couldn't handle the curriculum, but as a highly gifted child, she was completely bored with it. Unfortunately for us, no one knew what to do with her. We approached her teacher and the principal and were met with, "We really don't have the resources to support a child like yours. We could move her up several grades."

They had to be kidding me. Move her up? She was already the smallest kid in her second grade class and spoke with a slight lisp. She would be ostracized in a higher grade. It would be an emotional disaster. Something else had to be done.

My daughter needed emotional stability with academic challenges. But this combination was nearly impossible within the current framework of her school, which sought to teach and provide the bare basics—what was immediately needed to pass the next standardized test. Through lack of funding, many of their programs had been cut or reduced to a monochromatic scholastic environment; this clearly would not work for my wildly colorful child.

It was going to be left to me. I would need to think of things to challenge my seven-year-old. The last time I taught anything, it had been a theater class on Shakespeare at a local performing arts center several years earlier.

Shakespeare. Brilliant! I would create a lesson on Shakespeare's *Hamlet* for her. Heck, why stop there? Why not see if the school would allow me to teach it after school? Maybe this would spark something in these kids—if *she* wasn't challenged, there might be more kids like her. I would obviously need to do other traditional academic enrichment with Quinn too, but initially I had to open her up to learning again.

I worked continuously until I had a fully developed proposal: Shakespeare geared toward second graders. *Hamlet* could be intense and dark, but I found that it could be adapted for children fairly well. It had all of the elements of a good story: royalty, love, power, ghosts, dramatic sword fights, a mystery to be solved, and a great lesson on how revenge doesn't pay. Certainly this would hold the children's attention while introducing them to theater. Presenting it to the administration, I was really excited—excited for these kids, for exposing them to something so classic and enriching. My excitement was met with a very different response.

The principal, Mr. Rodriguez, sat there, his reading glasses balanced on his nose. Clearing his throat, he glanced at Mrs. Miller and then back at me.

"Mrs. Ellis, we see that you've put a lot of effort into this, but we are concerned that this is a bit . . . well, hmmm . . . a bit advanced for second graders."

The idea of Shakespeare might seem advanced—frankly I knew adults who were intimidated by Shakespeare. But having grown up in theater, I also knew that someone could come to grow and love his work and, like many things, it was all in how it was taught to you.

"Mr. Rodriguez, I understand that Shakespeare can be intimidating, but I think if presented and taught in the right way, it can be extremely beneficial to the student population. Shakespeare's writing gave birth to thousands of words and phrases we use today. His sonnets helped give structure to the English language. His plays are great examples of plot and characterization—all elements that the children will learn in their language arts classes. Through reading and understanding Shakespeare's stories, the children will be exposed to fundamentals of human nature. Yes, his words can be intellectually challenging, but that is precisely why this is an excellent enrichment activity. It will encourage the kids to reach out of their comfort zones and explore their boundaries—and when they are successful they will be able to feel an immense sense of accomplishment."

I studied his face and wanted to scream, *Maybe, just maybe it may light something in a child, other than mine, and get them to see that the world is beyond just what the state says they need to pass their standardized tests*, but I refrained. The key here was getting him to see the educational benefit without insulting how I thought the school was being run.

Seeing that he was on the fence, I added, "If you look

through my proposal, you can see that other schools from all over the world are successfully introducing Shakespeare—starting with children as young as the second grade, like I am proposing."

Although the initial meeting didn't go as planned, eventually, with teacher support, I was able to get my program approved. I offered to teach Shakespeare twice a week as an after-school program for anyone who was interested. It wouldn't be graded; it would be nothing but *fun* education. I didn't want to get paid; I just wanted to excite the children.

The program began slowly but very shortly gained momentum. What the administrators didn't realize was that the children didn't *know* that Shakespeare was complicated or intense. As a result, they didn't approach it with a "can't do" attitude. They only knew it was drama and was fun.

As the group of children and I worked through *Hamlet*, different things began to happen. There were lively discussions about the characters and the story. Kids began working together as they read through the scenes, forming new friendships and bonds. The students studied the words and became excited as they read the text correctly out loud. In Quinn it sparked something in her and she started engaging again in school.

At the end of the year, there was such positive feedback from the teachers and parents that other enrichment programs began to pop up. I guess my "crazy" idea had merit after all.

If your child is having educational issues, then take action.
Find another way if you have to. Don't be afraid to push the envelope.
Sometimes you can't get what you want or need for your kid
unless you get involved and possibly even do it yourself.

Growing with Anger
and Grief

*Colleen's Missing Pages: When a parent has died
and your child is grieving*

LIAM SAT ON THE FLOOR reading his *Boys' Life*, a scouting magazine. Carrying the laundry past him, I struggled to navigate the piles of toys, clothes, and other items strewn across his bedroom floor. On top of his dresser sat a picture of his father, Paul, who died of ALS (Lou Gehrig's disease) when Liam was just an infant. Pausing for a moment, I looked down to my now-seven-year-old son. Liam's light brown hair was wavy, as his father's had been.

I closed the last drawer and then said, "Liam, you need to pick up this stuff and clean your room. It's a mess in here."

No response.

Turning and fully facing him, I continued, "Liam, did you hear me? I said you need to clean up your room."

Liam rotated his face up toward me. His eyes were cold; hostility radiated from him.

"Why? It's not important, Mom."

"Liam, I'm not going to argue with you. You have a responsibility to take care of your things, to take care of this room."

Suddenly Liam pulled his arm back and launched the magazine, its pages fluttering as it flew past me.

"I'm not going to do it and you can't make me!" Liam's large frame sat unmoving on the floor.

"What's going on? Why are you acting like this? Why are you so upset? I just asked you to clean your room," I said as I knelt down and put my hands on his broad shoulders.

In the next moment there was a sharp pain in my stomach as his foot kicked me away.

"LIAM!"

I stopped myself. It was happening again—the same cycle as three weeks ago. But this was different. The level of anger was more intense.

Although I had been through some of this with Melissa, at about the same age as Liam was now, somehow it was different with her—maybe because she was a girl. Or perhaps it was because she had been four years old when Paul died. Melissa at least had memories of her "sit-down daddy," who had been in a wheelchair for most of his life with her.

But Liam? He was only three months old when Paul died. He had no memories of his father. To him Paul was a mosaic formed through other people's memories and pictures. But his construction of his father was lacking—deficient in his personal connection and at times without reality, because in his mind the dad he had created would never fuss at him to tidy his room or discipline him at all. In his mind, Paul was perfect.

Taking a deep breath, I said, "It's okay to be angry. It's not okay to kick Mommy because you are angry, but it's okay to be angry. We'll talk more when you can get control of yourself."

Standing, I turned to walk out of the bedroom. Before I reached the door, I heard Liam's voice.

"Why did you kill Daddy?"

I froze. This was a new one. Then, before I could turn around: "Why did you let Daddy die?"

Gently closing the door, I turned and looked at him and said, as calmly as possible, "That's not what happened. I did everything I could to keep him here. God decided it was his time to go."

Before I could continue, Liam interrupted. His gray eyes grew dark with contempt, his arms crossed over his chest. "Well, I don't like God. I think. I think I hate God. And I don't understand why you didn't die instead of him."

Another new one.

Contemplating what to say next, I looked past Liam to the picture of Paul that Liam kept on his dresser. Inside I screamed, *Who are you to leave me here alone? Why am I left to handle all of this?*

My internal rage with Paul was broken by the sounds of my seven-year-old's sobs.

I leaned into him and held him in my arms. Rocking him back and forth, I kissed him on his head. Between the sobs I heard a small, "I'm soooo sorry, Mom. I don't want you to die. I just want a dad."

"It's okay, Liam. It's all right to be angry. Anger is an emotion and you're allowed to feel it. And you know what? God is pretty tough. God can take it; he understands. He understands that you are trying to make sense of Daddy dying. It's normal to feel what you are feeling."

After I calmed Liam down, I left him to be alone in his room. Making my way into the kitchen, I needed a moment to think. The recent weeks had brought little eruptions of emotion from Liam, but nothing like the angered outburst that I had witnessed today. I couldn't think of any triggers, but there *had* to be something.

While waiting for some epiphany, I made myself a cup of tea with milk and sat down at the kitchen table. I flipped through my index of memories, incidents—anything I could think of related to Liam over the last few weeks. The only thing of significance that I recalled was a Cub Scouts meeting where Liam wanted me to leave him, specifically saying, "Mommy, please don't come, it's just for guys." He was less than thrilled when I, the only mother in the room, was obligated to stay, because he needed an adult with him. Unfortunately, that was all I could think of—and that was weeks ago. I couldn't believe that this alone was the trigger.

The house still quiet, I called a friend I had made while we were at hospice years before, when Paul died. Hospice, and Barbara specifically, had been lifesavers for me. Even though hospice was supposed to be only for the first year after Paul's death, I found they were still a resource that I could turn to.

Grateful to reach Barbara, I ran through the past few weeks of small eruptions as well as today's more anger-filled outburst. She reminded me that the anger could be rooted in a specific trigger or it could be as simple as Liam's recognizing that he is different from his friends, that he doesn't have a father like they do. I knew outbursts were expected, usually appear during different developmental milestones, and could continue for years after the parent's death. However, I was a little caught off guard because this one didn't appear to be tied to any specific thing.

I had done all I knew how to help my son. "Now what? What else can I do?"

"Colleen, all you can do is to try to communicate and get to the root of what is causing the outburst. It won't prevent the next one, but clear communication and permission to be angry or upset gives the child the space that he needs to work through his emotions."

"I know. I know. I am trying all of that, but I can't seem to get to the root of the problem."

"Why don't you bring him in to one of the hospice sessions? If he is willing to come, maybe he'll open up to one of us and talk about Paul. Talk to someone other than his mother about what he's feeling."

Grateful for her extension of help, I said we would come.

After that day, Liam spent some time at hospice and the outbursts retreated, but I expect the anger will flare up again. Until then I work through each day, ever conscious of the hole left by Paul's death. I try to expose my kids to positive male role models, and I try to anticipate possible triggers—knowing I will never be prepared for all of them.

Most important, however, I am working on deepening my relationship with Liam and Melissa. To have the open communication necessary for them to navigate their grief, they need to feel like they can come to me freely. The only way to have that type of relationship is to work on it and really be *present* for my kids. The laundry and dishes can wait until a little later; a moment with them on a spring day, running around playing ball in the yard, shouldn't have to.

Be aware that the grieving process continues for years after a parent dies . . . or after any major loss. To maintain the lines of communication with your child, focus on deepening your relationship with them. If there is an angry outburst, seek to understand what is driving your child's behavior because it may be an expression of grief. If your child won't share their emotions with you, see if they will speak to an outside family member, friend, or counselor about their feelings.

There Is No Easter Bunny

*Brea's Missing Pages: When a child
questions magical traditions*

IN THE DARKNESS, my minivan was uncharacteristically quiet. In front of me were miles of red taillights, the glow of which made me think of the strings of Christmas lights we would be hanging this Friday—as was our post-Thanksgiving tradition.

Glancing up in my rearview mirror, I watched as the bodies of my two youngest children, ages six and three, contorted in their seats, heads drooped and chests gently rising up and down. Jeff, my eight-year-old, was not asleep but rather seemed off in the distance, looking instead at the unmoving scenery around us.

"Mommmmm." A screeched whisper traveled up from the seat behind mine.

"Yes?"

"You know that there's no Easter Bunny?" Jeff whispered.

Alarmed the others might hear, I toned my voice to his level. "What are you talking about, Jeff?"

His body squirmed in his seat. He caught my eye in the rearview mirror and then turned to look at his siblings. In a low whisper he said, "Good, they're asleep," and connected once again with my eyes.

"Why's that good?"

"Well. . . ."

He smiled an impish *I know something you don't know* smile.

"Well what, Jeff? What are you talking about? Who told you that?"

"Wellllll. Remember at Easter when we were at Grandma's house and our cousins were there too?" He bit his lip, unsure if he should tell me everything. "Ah, well, Troy said, 'You shouldn't believe that story, 'cause there's no Easter Bunny.'"

I could see it all unfolding. His ten-year-old cousin had told him there was no Easter Bunny, and now that we were approaching Christmas, he was beginning to question whether there was a Santa Claus. I knew that I had to choose my words carefully because the other two children might wake up at any time. If Jeff no longer wanted to believe, I was fine with that, but I didn't want to ruin the magic for my younger children.

The question was really how to respond. Was Jeff merely testing me? If so, I didn't want to destroy what little time he had left believing in something magical, *but* I also really didn't want to lie. Although it was a fine line, I always had sought ways to be truthful in everything that I said to my children. The question was in finding that balance.

"Jeff, I think it comes down to what *you* believe. I remember when I was a little girl and right before Easter I woke up in the middle of the night and swore I saw the Easter Bunny. It made me scared that a giant bunny was staring at me, and I pulled my covers over my head. I wouldn't pull them back down because

I thought if the bunny saw me awake I wouldn't get an Easter basket. I slept all night like that. The next morning I found a basket left for me."

By the time I had finished my tale, I saw the sleep-heavy eyes of my two youngest looking up at me. Luckily they did not appear to be fully awake and Jeff, for now, went off to staring at the automotive landscape around us.

Families handle magical traditions differently; some may not believe in them at all. Some of this is rooted in varying religions and even in different Christian upbringings. Inherently I knew all of this, but I had hoped that if my children ran into someone who didn't share our views, that person would at least respect our desire to maintain our magical traditions. I want my children to hold on to the magic as long as possible—because this world they are living in has precious little magic left.

It simply didn't make sense that Troy would try to spoil it for his cousins. Maybe Troy had simply reached an age where logic had surpassed magic—I only wished he had the common sense not to spoil it for his younger cousins. If he didn't believe, and my sister-in-law Helen knew, one would have thought she would have advised him to keep it quiet. Which made me wonder, did Helen know he no longer believed?

That evening I brought up the subject with my husband, Randy, putting him in charge of the delicate phone call to his sister. Helen's shock on the other end of the phone line was felt by both of us. She didn't know Troy no longer believed, or at least said he no longer believed. Hanging up the phone, Randy turned to me.

"She's gonna talk to him. She sounded very sad, Brea."

As silly as it seems, a certain level of grief hung in the air. If Troy no longer believed in the Easter Bunny, Santa, or the Tooth Fairy, then truly we didn't have much time left with our own children—time to watch them believe that the world was still a magical place.

I thought of Helen as she sat Troy down, trying to navigate the waters of what he believed. Later she told me that when the subject of the conversation with Jeff came up between them, Troy had cried because he knew he shouldn't have said anything that might ruin it for Jeff. Helen thought perhaps part of the issue was that Troy was sad that the magic was gone for him and didn't want others to have what he didn't have anymore.

Truly I wasn't angry with Troy; instead, I felt a little sad for him. I remembered how upsetting it was for me to realize the truth when I was a child, because I wanted to keep believing that magic could exist in someplace other than in movies or fairy tales. I also felt bad for Helen because as a parent, when you get to see your child delight in magical traditions, a certain amount of the joy you felt as a child returns. The childhood innocence would be gone for her now, existing only as memories or in family photos.

As Christmas approached, Randy and I held our breath. We didn't know how much Jeff still believed. Throughout early to mid-December we looked for negative signs; luckily there weren't any. The real test was Christmas morning, when he came bounding down the stairs with his brother and sister. Jeff ran into the family room ahead of his siblings, where the tree was lit and surrounded by presents. Seeing it, he exclaimed, "Santa came!" We knew then, at least for now, there was still magic.

There are ways to be honest and still maintain the magic.
Each family has to decide how they will handle magical traditions
in a way that not only preserves what they want for their children,
but also is respectful to other people's beliefs.

The Flip of a Switch

Patricia's Missing Pages: When a child just doesn't seem to care about his future

"BY GOD, PATRICIA, he's almost eighteen—he isn't a child anymore. He *needs* to get it together."

"Andrew, he isn't some young Marine like you were. He is . . . different. You *know* that."

"Well, the military is good for discipline, and I know that they are talking about bringing back the draft—especially with this business in Iraq. Turn on the TV; I want to hear what President Bush has to say."

Leaning over, I turned on the television and stoked the fire. Somehow this January night seemed just a little bit colder. I couldn't believe it was 1991, that my son would graduate from high school this year, and that a war was on the horizon. We were going to war for the first time since Vietnam. Memories of young friends of mine being drafted flooded my mind: friends, almost the same age as my son, who had never come back from that unwinnable war.

I heard Jeremy's footsteps behind me. His eyes were affixed to the sight of men in full desert gear walking through the distorted waves of heat. He was silent as we all listened.

"No president can easily commit our sons and daughters to war. They are the nation's finest. Ours is an all-volunteer force, magnificently trained, highly motivated. . . ." Bush's authoritative voice continued.

"I wonder how long it will be voluntary," I said, echoing Andrew's earlier sentiments.

I only hoped that Jeremy was listening. That maybe, just maybe, he would think about what was coming next. For so long I had hoped that something, anything might "flip his switch" and we would see him try or be excited about something . . . anything.

The speech ended and Jeremy disappeared again into his room.

I turned the TV off and sat there thinking about our son. From the time he was a little boy, he was delightful and extremely bright but never appeared to be motivated. He just didn't seem to care about anything—friends, school, sports, anything. No one could explain it, not the teachers, not his principal—no one.

I remember that when Jeremy was in the fourth grade, I met with the principal, Mr. Perry, and watched as this *authority*, with years of educational experience, looked defeated.

"We can't pinpoint anything wrong with Jeremy. From an aptitude level, it appears he is able to do most of the work; he just refuses to engage. Nothing motivates him academically. I've never seen anything like it." Mr. Perry's shoulders slumped as if the effort to motivate and "fix" my son had drawn all of the energy from him.

As if to offer some consolation, he continued, "At least he doesn't appear to be psychologically damaged. Patricia, trust me when I say you never want to experience *that*. What you are dealing with is rough, but it's horrible for parents whose kids have psychological issues."

Initially I think they had wanted to blame it on me, because I was a working professional, an anomaly in the small southern town in which we lived in. In our town, women were expected to stay home and be nothing more than a homemaker. Therefore, if my son was deficient, then I was somehow at fault because I had a career. Over time, however, Jeremy's teachers and even Mr. Perry began to recognize that although I worked, my son came first and I had tried everything to motivate him to care about his schoolwork.

No matter where I turned, there were suggestions for me. "Create a good work environment" was one; consequently, we stripped his room of all playthings and set up a study area. Jeremy simply sat there. He didn't want to work, or read, or do anything. We tried time-outs for refusing to do work and rewards for completed homework. Still nothing changed. Then there were years of field trips and enrichment activities, in the hope that one of these might excite him. Nothing worked. The only thing he remotely showed interest in was tinkering at home with anything mechanical or electrical, but these types of activities didn't show up in school.

Ironically, as much as he didn't engage at school, either academically or socially, he never seemed to mind going. I couldn't understand how he could be punctual for class but at the same time put no energy into completing the homework or studying for it.

Periodically we took him for tests only to find that there was nothing wrong with him; he was incredibly bright but simply lacked the desire to do any schoolwork. His ability to listen well during classes allowed him to absorb just enough information that if he was called on he could talk through an answer, but if you asked him to write that same answer down for an assignment it wouldn't happen.

What was amazing was that he simply did not care what anyone thought; he would freely tell other children about this meeting or that meeting or tests where they were trying to figure out what was "wrong" with him. When visiting friends or family asked how school was going and if he liked it, Jeremy would respond, "I like it, but I'm not doing well. They don't think I work hard enough."

Finally, at the conference with Mr. Perry in the fourth grade, we simply accepted that this was Jeremy and there was nothing we could do but love and support him for who he was, albeit completely unmotivated. Secretly I harbored the dream that someday he would find something, and when we relocated up north I thought he might have.

When Jeremy was in high school, we moved to a more urban, diverse area outside Philadelphia. Here I began to see what all my field trips and enrichment activities had failed to accomplish—a small glimmer of light behind his eyes. He actually began to study, but because he had spent many years not doing so, he realized at points that he "didn't get it" because he hadn't retained basic, foundational knowledge, yet he still pushed on. His efforts infused hope within me, until this, his senior year. Only a few weeks ago during the holiday break we sat in the dining room and talked about his future.

Leaning his chair back, balanced carefully on the rear two legs, Jeremy grasped his hands behind his head, a wide grin spread across his face. "Pretty soon I won't have to go to school at all." The hope I had held for him to continue this positive streak suddenly came to a familiar halt.

"Would you consider vocational school?" I asked—desperate

to find him something to work toward.

"Nah. I really don't want to go to school at all."

My anxiety was rising all over again. I really didn't care what Jeremy did, but I wanted to make sure that he could support himself, and I knew that having a college degree or some type of vocational program was key. But like so many times before, he simply did not seem to care.

As the frigid January wind blew outside, I sat there by the fire wondering how Jeremy could walk away, seemingly unaffected by the president's speech. I don't know what my hopes were for tonight. I hoped that maybe the thought of the draft, of being forced into the military, might spur my son into action. At this point I'd completely run out of ideas.

The following morning, Jeremy came down for breakfast. The sun streaming through the window did little to warm us against the cold. As he walked into the kitchen I saw him carrying a stack of papers. He pushed them to the side and drank his juice.

"Jeremy, what's all that?" I asked, taking a long sip of my coffee.

"Just college applications. I'm going to go to college. Think I want to be an accountant."

Startled, I gasped and nearly choked on my hot coffee. Excusing myself, I cleaned the coffee off my chin and, steeling myself against the kitchen counter, regained my composure. Shock and panic hit me at the same time. Fearful I might say the wrong thing and scare him off, I turned and simply said, "That's great, honey."

By spring Jeremy was accepted into one of the colleges he had applied to. For the next several years, Jeremy diligently attended classes and eventually sat for and passed his CPA.

I believe that the sudden and dramatic change the morning after the president's speech resulted from learning that he might be drafted sometime in the near future, which helped flip the switch in my son. He has never admitted to this, and to this day I don't know if there were other contributing factors. However, one thing is clear: choosing to engage in life had to be on Jeremy's own terms.

Inspiration and motivation can be found in the oddest of places. Or they can just arrive from out of nowhere . . . by surprise. Continue to love and support your child, and eventually the switch may just turn on all by itself.

Sensory System Overload

*Meg's Missing Pages: When you see
a problem where others don't*

WE WERE ALL ASSEMBLED, the entire Frazier family including the patriarch, dressed in reds, greens, and whites. The outfits were perfectly coordinated—down to hair bows and ties for the little ones. Their easy smiles exuded comfortable confidence. It would be a beautiful family photo, but for one thing—my daughter.

"Meg," my sister called to me, "can't you get Michelle over here? It'll be a quick photo, we promise." The rest was left unsaid. This was probably our last chance to get a family photo with Poppy, because he had been given only a few months to live. Yet once again I knew I would not be able to get my four-year-old daughter to comply.

Turning toward the crowd, I implored them, "Please just take it without us."

My response was met with bewildered stares. They simply could not understand; in our family, everything is orderly and performed well, and any deviation from that is foreign. My daughter's behavior is foreign to them.

Briefly Michelle looked at them, the fear evident in her green eyes. Attempting to get outside their reach, Michelle turned and tripped.

The wailing began in earnest.

Careful not to touch her too much, I ushered her out of the room. Turning back toward the group, I said, "You're going to have to take the photo without her. *Please* take it without her."

I watched as she sat there, withdrawn from me, in her beautiful knit dress adorned with holly leaves, her bright red bow resting against her mass of chocolate curls, screaming in apparent pain. My frustration grew as I could not find evidence of an injury that would warrant the level of screaming coming from her. Still worse, there was nothing I could do to console my daughter.

Too many past experiences had taught me that we needed simply to wait it out.

Although Michelle outwardly looked normal, I knew that she wasn't; I knew something was notably different about her. Later, during the hourlong drive home from the "Christmas Disaster," instead of the passing scenery, I saw flashbacks of Michelle's young life.

At two years old, I noticed that Michelle didn't respond as other children did. Her tantrums were often unprovoked and took hours to recover from. When I mentioned it in passing to my parents and sisters, and even my pediatrician, they brushed it aside: "She's young; she'll grow out of it." Being new parents, my ex-husband and I hoped they were right.

Shortly after Michelle turned three, there was another incident. It was her younger sister Ava's first birthday and the house was full of family and close friends. Again there were the attempts at getting the "perfect photo." Only that time, the tantrum resulted in Michelle tearing off her clothes and running into the home office to escape. I found her there cowering under a desk like a caged animal.

Visiting the pediatrician's office, I once again shared my experiences with the doctors. "I know it's normal for kids to have temper tantrums at this age, but they're so extreme and so profound, I really think something else is going on." No matter how many times I expressed these concerns, the response was always, "Don't worry. She'll grow out of it."

Now at four, she had still not grown out of it. Rather, it was beginning to escalate. The "Christmas Disaster" was the second significant episode in little more than a month. The list of items that would trigger the outbursts was also growing. Each time, she would seek to withdraw from everyone, and consoling her would only intensify the situation. Instinctively I wanted to hold her in my arms and protect her, but I began to learn through experience that something as small as my touch could be painful to her. I had to fight what came naturally and do what I knew she needed from me—which was to simply watch her work through her pain until she had calmed enough that I could approach. Instead of holding her, I would speak calmly at a distance. I would offer reassurances that I was there but was going to allow her to calm down and regroup.

There had to be an answer. This was not normal. I couldn't bear to watch my child spiral further out of control. In the week between Christmas and New Year's, I began to investigate possible sources for Michelle's issues in earnest. Having a medical background as a nurse, I was somewhat familiar with something called sensory integration dysfunction (SID). Basically, the sensory information we receive every day (visual, auditory, tactile, etc.) is interpreted and processed differently by the brain with someone with SID. What may appear as a *normal* sound or experience to a regularly functioning person may actually be felt as *painful* to a person with SID. One common and observable issue is with textures. A person with SID often has problems with the textures of certain foods. In Michelle's case, she had issues with the texture of broccoli.

When Michelle was a baby, she would eat all sorts of foods—including broccoli. Later, when I tried to serve it to her steamed, we had an episode of sorts. Michelle had taken a bit of the softened, steamed stem and eaten it without issue. But when she tried to consume the treelike top of the broccoli, she spat it out. Using her fingers she desperately sought to remove all the flowery particles left on her tongue. At first I thought it strange, especially since she'd eaten it without issue before. Then I realized it wasn't an issue with the flavor, but rather that the texture of the broccoli top which was the root of the problem. It was another example of her heightened sensitivity to something that most consider normal.

Thinking I might have determined a potential source of my daughter's problems, I returned to the pediatrician's office, shared my concerns with the doctors, and asked if I should take her to be evaluated by some type of specialist. The response, like multiple times before, was lukewarm. "Oh, well, since you feel that way, you can go have it checked out and let's see what they say." The doctors finally referred me to an occupational therapist.

The first occupational therapist evaluated Michelle and concluded that there were some relevant indicators, like the low grip strength in her hands—abnormal for a child of her age. Other than that, they did not find anything else.

There it was. There was nothing really wrong with my daughter. A part of me wanted to trust that and believe I had overreacted. The realistic part of me knew I simply had not found the answer yet.

I wanted a second opinion. After I spent some time searching and asking around, the name of a particular occupational therapist kept reappearing. The problem? I knew her as "Addison's mom," because Addison was one of the few friends Michelle felt comfortable with. As much as I wanted to uncover the source of Michelle's problems, I was equally concerned about alienating one of the few friends she had. My daughter had already been turned away by other friends because she was *different*, and I guess I was scared it might be awkward if Melanie, Addison's mom, began treating Michelle—that perhaps Addison might treat Michelle differently because she was one of her mother's patients and not just a friend from school.

The appointment I made next was probably one of the best things I ever did for Michelle. Determined to get another opinion, and hopefully some answers, I called Melanie and set up an evaluation. While preparing for the evaluation, Melanie had me fill out a questionnaire about Michelle and her behavior. As I answered the questions, it became increasingly apparent to me that there was a pattern emerging with my answers. I didn't know what the pattern meant entirely but was confident there was something to my gut instinct that things weren't right.

At the end of March I found myself pulling up to Addison and Melanie's house. "Michelle, we're going to see Miss Melanie, Addison's mommy, today."

I looked at her. Instead of angst, I saw calmness and happiness in her eyes. A weight was partially lifted.

For the next several hours Miss Melanie evaluated Michelle. Melanie was a true professional and had a way of disarming Michelle; as a result, what unfolded was as close to Michelle's true behavior as I could expect during an evaluation. Even if I couldn't discern anything from Melanie's responses, I felt like Michelle was truly—perhaps really for the first time—getting thoroughly analyzed. At the end of the evaluation, she allowed

Michelle and Addison some playtime so we might speak.

"Meg, I'll write up a formal evaluation, but I want you to know that Michelle's results give us several areas of concern. In addition to the grip strength issue, she also seems to have neck and trunk weakness, which need to be addressed. Michelle demonstrated abnormal responses to bright lights and certain sound frequencies. There are also pain regulation issues. In conjunction with the full report, I am going to put together a plan of therapies we can use to help her better respond to these stimuli as well increase the strength in the physical areas where she is deficient." Melanie was direct and professional, her eyes intently focused on me and my response.

Hearing Melanie's words, I wanted to cry. It was as if for the first time in years my voice had been heard, my instincts validated. Looking over, I saw Michelle and Addison playing like two normal little girls; in that moment I knew there was hope for my daughter. Perhaps equally important, Addison didn't appear to be treating Michelle any differently than she had before when they'd played.

Over the next year, Michelle went through several hours of occupational therapy each week at Melanie's home. She also had "homework," which I had to do with her at home each day to better sensitize her to surrounding stimuli. I engaged the whole family, including her cousins if they were over, and tried to make it seem more like a game than a chore.

Now, at six, Michelle's issues are not solved, but she is much better able to cope with the sensory stressors around her. The pediatrician's office was notified, and even if they didn't place much relevancy on it, I know the proof is in the everyday behavior of my daughter. Having a diagnosis or label, we were also able to more clearly explain to our extended family the challenges that Michelle faces. With this information, I feel my family is now more equipped to grasp Michelle's issues. That understanding and her progress with occupational therapy has enabled her to function more like her peers. Much to my delight, Michelle will now pose for and smile in pictures.

The experience has taught me a lot, not only about this disorder but about how to be a better parent. If you persevere, you eventually will get the answers that you need. Understanding your child and any challenges they may have will allow you to more effectively parent them.

More than anything, it taught me to have compassion and understanding for other parents. Sometimes what we observe superficially is not reality; rather than judge, we should seek to understand what difficulties that parent may be facing.

Trust your instincts; your heart will lead you past where your mind stops. Don't be afraid to question the "authorities." The sooner you can catch issues, the more likely your child can be helped and deficient areas developed. More important, the sooner you know what you are dealing with, the sooner you will be able to be a more effective parent.

Take a Deep Breath and Redirect

Carolina's Missing Pages: When a child is just as stubborn as you are

"SOPHIA, YOU CAN'T HAVE THAT, it has too much sugar in it," I said, cradling Gabriella on my hip.

"Mama, I don't want anything else—I want that *cupcake!*" Sophia stomped her three-year-old foot and pointed to the chocolate delight capped in two inches of gleaming white frosting in the pastry case.

The frustration was rising. Recently it seemed like every day Sophia was challenging me. I would say, "Go right," and she would go left, repeatedly doing what she wanted to do over what I told her to do. This was enough. An elevated response escaped my mouth: "I said no!"

Sophia glared up at me with her dark brown eyes—my eyes—unwavering.

Without turning around, I could feel my mother staring at me, watching what amounted to a Colombian standoff between my daughter and me. My mother gracefully stepped between us and guided Sophia toward another section of the glass case.

"Sophia, do you see what they have here? They have little banana muffins on a plate with strawberries. Don't they look cute?"

"Yes, *mi abuela*." Sophia turned her face toward my mother, a smile spreading across her face. A matching, not quite smug smile, spread across my mother's.

"Sir, we will take the banana muffin plate, an orange juice, and two lattes, please." I ordered before Sophia had a chance to change her mind.

With the tray of coffees and the muffin precariously balanced, we walked over to a table for four in the back of the coffee shop.

Sitting across from my mother, I observed in amazement as my daughter devoured the banana muffin and strawberries she had previously scorned. My thoughts were interrupted by . . .

"She's like you. Strong-headed."

Tell me something I don't know.

"*Caro*, you need to figure out a way for *you* to adjust when this happens. Redirect or distract her. Be smarter. Otherwise the two of you will battle back and forth and you'll get nowhere."

As much as I hated to admit it, there was truth and wisdom in what my mother was saying. I have always been stubborn, and Sophia, unfortunately for me, *was* just like me. Each time we got into a disagreement, I would continue to engage her, pushing back, until a full-blown standoff ensued and I was forced to put her in a time-out. Sometimes Sophia acted like she didn't care; other times she'd throw a fit—screaming and kicking. We were both stubborn, but my continued attempts to engage her, to change her response, were not working. Sophia was only a kid; instead of trying to force her to change, maybe I just needed to change my approach.

Honestly, I was also irritated that Sophia's behavior had gotten worse while my mother was visiting from Colombia. I don't know why it happens, but there must be some universal law that says when you have company visiting—especially your parents—things must go awry. Adding insult to injury, I also knew that my mother's observations were probably right. At minimum there had to be a better way, because time-outs alone were simply not working—for either of us.

I finished my latte with a resolve to try what my mother had suggested and not rely on my "stubborn" nature. Strangely I was contented by the thought of a new approach. I didn't like it when Sophia and I fought. Sometimes I had visions of her being a teenager and us having similar standoffs. I didn't want that type of relationship with my daughter, now or in the future. My mother was an insightful woman and one who knew me well. I was hopeful that her approach would be what my daughter and I needed.

The next day Sophia was sulking because she wanted to go to the park. I had said no because Gabriella, my six-month-old, was napping.

"But I wanna go to the park NOW, Mamma!"

My body tensed instantly.

This time it would be different. Instead of going to battle with her, I took a deep breath and, scanning the room, saw the finger paints and paper.

"Sophia, you really shouldn't talk to me that way. Now let's see what else we could do. Hmmm, if I recall, you used to like to paint, but I don't know if you are up to it."

I turned away slightly, but I saw her studying me and my response. This time, instead of battling with me, she slid over toward the paints.

"Mama, can I paint?" she said, holding the tube of green finger paint.

"Sophia, that's a great idea. Sure!"

With that, I spread out the paper and remaining paints. For the next half hour I sat smiling as Sophia smeared the colors all over the paper. We had finally gotten through a confrontation without a standoff or time-outs. I found that containing my emotional, stubborn nature was far more effective at getting Sophia to do what I wanted than forcing my will onto her. As my mother would say, I became *smarter* in how I parented Sophia.

Like our children, we, too, can be stubborn or simply stuck on one method of parenting. Sometimes it is best to take a breath, redirect, and be flexible enough to try a new approach.

Staying Calm in the
Face of Upset

*Kelly's Missing Pages: When little disasters threaten
to ruin your good intentions*

THE CAR WAS PACKED and we were finally on our way, driving away from L.A. for a mini-vacation. I felt free, freer than I had in a long time. My divorce from Kurt was now final, and I'd decided I was going to get my kids, Mason and Jackson, out of the city and expose them to one of the most beautiful places in the world: Yosemite National Park.

Truth be told, I didn't really know much about Yosemite, much less camping. But this was my personal challenge. I was taking my two boys camping, on my own, without a man around. Reveling in my independence, I didn't notice that the car had begun to ride differently, and I kept driving north on the Grapevine. By the time I noticed it, we were two hours into our trip.

Then Mason, with his wise eight years of age, pointed out the obvious. "Uh, why is there smoke coming out from under the hood?"

My eyes moved from the rearview mirror to my hood. Smoke slowly billowed out of each side. *Oh no! I can't break down; we're not even halfway there!* This was my time to do it right, not break down on the side of the road.

Ahead of me I saw the sign for Buttonwillow—population 1,500. Amazingly enough, in that town of 1,500, I knew people—my former in-laws. I really hoped I wouldn't have to call them for help.

Nursing my car along, I managed to get it to a service station. After a few hours they determined my issue: I had blown a head gasket. This car was going absolutely *nowhere.*

So much for not calling my former in-laws.

The service station looked as if it were frozen in the 1970s. My boys sat in orange plastic bucket chairs, watching a small TV, as I stepped outside to call my former in-laws.

"Hey, Marybeth, it's Kelly."

"Why, this is a surprise. How've you been?"

"We've been well. The boys and I were actually on our way to Yosemite when we broke down, in Buttonwillow of all places."

"Oh, no. Where exactly are you now? Can Dale and I help you?"

"Actually that's why I'm calling; could you watch the boys while I find a rental car?"

Marybeth paused a moment before responding, "Are you going to try to continue with the trip?"

Maybe they thought I was crazy for pushing on, but I wasn't going to let this issue derail our trip—not if I could find a rental car and still make it happen.

Hoping to bypass further questioning, I added, "That's the plan! Right now we're over at Danny's Automotive Repair. If you are able to pick the boys up from here, it would be great."

"No problem at all; it will be great to see them. If it turns out you need to stay for dinner or something, know that you're welcome here."

"Thanks for the offer. I hope we won't need it, but I appreciate it."

The boys safely with my in-laws, I set out to find a rental car. I couldn't believe it. I mean, here I was, a single mom trying to take my boys on vacation, spending hundreds of dollars I didn't have on a weekly rental car and thousands more to repair my beat-up car. But *we were going on this vacation*. I was not going to fail and I figured if it had begun like this, then it was only destined to get better.

At least I told myself that.

By the time I'd retrieved the rental car and transferred our luggage to it, darkness had begun to descend and it didn't seem wise to press on that evening. As much as I hated to waste the day and *again* accept my in-laws' help, I acquiesced to Marybeth's offer to stay the night.

Turning toward my children with a smile—which I hoped disguised my frustration and instead conveyed a tone of *What a great adventure!*—I said, almost too brightly, "Looks like we're staying in Buttonwillow for the night!"

The following morning I stepped outside my in-laws' house to load our overnight bags back into the rental car. The bright, cheerful sun contrasted with the unease taking root in my stomach. The first night of my *independent* vacation had been anything but. I briefly wondered if this was a sign that we shouldn't go, but I pushed the doubt out of my mind.

When I turned to call to the boys, I saw them saying goodbye to their grandparents. I met their dubious looks with a forced smile and enthusiasm.

"Come on, boys! Let's get going to Yosemite!"

The boys made their way down to the car. All safely in the car, we backed out, issued one last farewell wave, and were once again on our way.

Along the winding roads I cracked jokes and played the requisite road trip games. I wanted them to have a trip they would remember, something that could be bantered about during holiday dinners: "Remember our trip to Yosemite?" At times, when we were all laughing together about something silly that we'd identified while playing I Spy, I thought maybe this trip would be something they might hold on to as a good childhood memory.

Immediately after lunch we pulled into the camping village within the park. After check-in, we carted our belongings from the designated parking area through the private streets of the Curry Village, the location of our tent cabin.

The uniform size and placement of the tent cabins reminded me of Monopoly houses, but these were not green but rather white canvas tents stretched out over permanent wooden frames, erected on top of modestly elevated platforms. Tightly packed in, the cabins were assembled in rows, each with two or three stairs leading from the cabin to the street. Adjacent to the stairs was a large metal box, which I knew from the brochures was for storing our food. Pulling the cart behind us, I looked for our tent number.

"Boys, look at the cabin doors for our tent number. We are tent 412. I think it should be on the right."

The boys spotted it before I did. They ran ahead of me as I pulled our cart to the front and parked it there temporarily.

Propping open the door to the tent, I surveyed the spacious room as my boys excitedly claimed their beds. It was perfect. Centered in the room was a single overhead light. Around it were four cots, with bedding and linens neatly folded at the foot of each. Not being a former Girl Scout, or anything close to that, I was grateful that I didn't have to worry about putting up a tent or sleeping on the ground. *Another small victory.*

After we got settled in, it was time for dinner. I had come prepared and pulled out my borrowed, minimalistic propane stove. Setting everything up in the picnic area, I thought, *I've got this.* The boys were seated at the other end of the table snacking on chips and watching me prepare dinner. Turning the flame on, I realized very soon that I couldn't control it. Focusing intently on not scorching the beans, I failed to notice the two-liter plastic bottle of soda standing next to the stove on the picnic table.

The next thing I knew there was an explosion. The bottle of soda shot up like a rocket, showering the three of us with sticky lemon-lime soda. The noise and soda rain brought with it a flurry of spectators running toward us, intent on investigating the source of the explosion.

"Hey, are you okay?" The look of concern of the man decked in full L.L. Bean gear was endearing as it was frustrating.

Wiping the lemon-lime spray from my face, I simply smiled and said, "Yeah. No problem. I just got the soda too close to the stove, I guess."

"Okay, well . . . let us know if you need any help with anything. We're staying in that tent right over there," the L.L. Bean model said before walking back to his perfectly ordered picnic table. I saw him look back at us once more as he explained, complete with hand gestures, to his wife what had happened. I could only imagine that conversation. ("Poor woman doesn't know what the hell she's doing.")

I turned back toward my two boys. They were sitting there silently. Watching. Watching to see what I would do next. I sat down with them and started laughing. Pretty soon all three of us, covered in sticky soda, were laughing under a canopy of the trees in the park.

The remainder of the trip continued to be filled with mishaps and near-mishaps. I wish I could say I documented it all, but unfortunately—or fortunately—even my camera died. I guess I should have known that would happen.

As we left the park I somehow figured we'd had our fill of misadventures. I was wrong.

Driving out of Yosemite Valley, we were forced to take the long, winding park road. Back and forth and back and forth we drove. After the first pass, I began to worry about my sons and how they were handling the curves, and then I heard it: the intake of breath right before vomiting.

Grabbing the plastic grocery bag from the front seat, I shook out the contents and flung the bag back to Mason just in time for him to hurl into it.

The putrid smell crept through the car despite my attempts to open the windows and air it out. Unfortunately we were on a stretch of the road where we couldn't pull over. Then I heard the sucking noise again, only this time it was Jackson, my six-year-old.

I looked to my seat and there was nothing but a mostly empty bag of popcorn. I grabbed it and threw it back to Jackson.

"Sorry, honey. You're gonna have to throw up on the popcorn. It's the only bag we have left, so you're just gonna have to use it."

The bag made it to him just in time. Looking back, I saw the vomit-coated bag of popcorn and it was all I could do not to throw up myself.

Through it all, surprisingly I was remarkably calm, and this set the tone for the boys. Despite throwing up and having a rather unpleasant trip home, they didn't freak out or get upset. Later, after we had stopped, cleaned up and were back on our way, the boys even fell asleep. As I looked back at them, my fingers loosened a bit around the steering wheel. Finally the relaxed demeanor that I had shown to the outside world now matched the peace I held inside. By focusing on trying to appear cool and collected, I somehow transitioned into actually being that way; maybe it was because they were asleep, but hey, I'll take what I can get.

So . . . the trip did not go well, or smoothly, or any of the things I had hoped for. But I had done it on my own and remained composed, despite being totally out of my comfort zone.

And we had fun amid our small disasters.

And it definitely created those "Remember our trip to Yosemite?" moments, even if they were not the type I had hoped for.

When I tell people about the trip, they seem surprised that I didn't pack up and just find some little hotel with a pool instead. My response has always been that at some point, you just have to realize that sometimes life is going to hand you less-than-ideal situations. It's our job as parents to create as calm an environment as possible for our kids—even if we are in crisis internally.

When things don't go according to your plan, build an environment where your kids can look to you and feel that "It's not a big deal . . . we will figure it out." Doing so will instill a relaxed confidence in them, which will ultimately help them deal with the unexpected twists and turns of the road trip of life.

Accidents Happen

Naomi's Missing Pages: When a child
is seriously ill or injured

IT WAS VALENTINE'S DAY and my boys, six and four years old, had just enjoyed a rare treat of chocolate. Over the next hour or so they danced around the living room. Sitting back, my husband and I watched their moves as they boogied and shook the sugar out of their systems. Jordan, our six-year-old, then tried to break-dance. I watched as Jordan put his head on the floor; right as he began to spin, he flipped over instead. He lay there sobbing, his body slightly twisted. As with any roughhousing event, it's all fun and games until someone gets hurt.

I picked Jordan up and held him for a few minutes. Convinced it was merely a minor mishap, I handed him to my husband, Patrick, following it with a direction to all the boys: "Okay, guys, that's it. Bedtime."

While Patrick put Jordan and Peter to bed, I went back to the kitchen and cleaned up. I disposed of the source of all the mayhem—the partially empty red-foil box of chocolates.

As I turned back toward the sink, Patrick walked into the kitchen.

"Naomi, Jordan's still crying. He said his neck hurts."

"All right, I'll go have a look. He probably simply strained a muscle." I dried my hands on the dish towel and walked back toward the bedrooms.

Before I could reach his door, Jordan's whimpers became apparent. "Hey, baby. What's wrong?" I said as I pushed his black hair back from his forehead.

"Mom, I think I hurt my neck."

"Don't worry, baby, just sit there and I'll try to massage it. I'll help you loosen it. Okay?"

"Okay, Mom," he said in a low, pained whisper.

As a physical therapist in an orthopedic practice, I had seen more than my fair share of sprains and performed manual manipulations on muscle spasms. Slowly and gently I massaged his neck in rhythm to the patterns of the animals that were being projected on his wall by his night light. A few minutes before he fell asleep, I gave him some Motrin.

Leaving him, I went about my evening routine of starting the dishwasher, cleaning up the house, and laying out all of the lunchboxes and things necessary for the next school day.

As I passed Jordan's door again, I observed him drifting in and out of sleep. He was clearly still uncomfortable. Trying to be cautious, I thought it best that I lay there beside him and check him again in a few hours. I set my alarm for one a.m., planning on reassessing the situation then.

I was not really asleep, so the initial chirp of my watch alarm woke me up completely. Jordan also was not completely sleeping. *The muscle spasms must be really rough*, I thought. I tried to touch him and adjust his head, and he started crying heavily again. Something was wrong. He obviously needed a more detailed evaluation and something beyond Motrin for his spasms. He needed to go to the ER, but if it could wait, I wanted him to be seen by someone at the beginning of the day shift rather than at the end of the night shift. Having worked in hospitals, I knew the toll a night shift could take on a practitioner.

Over the next few hours I dozed here and there, my body tense and alert to any of Jordan's movements or sounds. Before I knew it, it was around 6:30 a.m. and time to go the ER. Standing over Jordan's bed, I contemplated the best way to transport him. The contortions on his face gave me the direction I needed. There was simply no way to comfortably get him into a car seat. I would need to call the paramedics.

As I placed the call to 911, I ran around the house and gathered up things to take with us and for Jordan to do while we waited to be seen. Before leaving with the ambulance, I instructed Patrick to get Peter to school, thinking he could meet up with us in the ER later and take us home. I figured at most we might be there a few hours, because really I didn't think there was anything major to be concerned about.

When the paramedics arrived they stabilized Jordan's neck and carried him out to the ambulance. I kissed Patrick and Peter good-bye, with assurances that we'd see them again soon. Squeezing into the ambulance and around to where Jordan was positioned on a gurney, I sat opposite the paramedic, holding Jordan's hand, comforting him as they closed the doors and we drove away.

When we arrived at the ER, they wheeled us right back and into a curtained area. Within a few minutes, a nurse practitioner came in, triaged the situation, and ordered x-rays. While we waited, I adjusted the personal TV for Jordan to watch cartoons. A short time later, a nurse's aide came in to wheel Jordan's gurney down for his x-rays. I walked alongside, holding his hand.

"It's really cool. They take a special picture and it goes through your skin and you can see your bones! The only thing to remember is that you need to lie very still when they take them, okay? Otherwise they will turn out all blurry and we'll have to take them all over again."

"Okay, Mom," was all Jordan managed to muster.

Two hours after our initial arrival, Jordan and I were back to our curtained examining room. The x-rays had been taken, and now we were waiting on the results. I saw the doctor pull back the curtain, and Patrick walked in right behind him.

"Mrs. Walters, Mr. Walters? I'm Dr. Warfield and I will be treating your son today." The doctor was holding Jordan's chart and films in his hands, and somehow I knew he had more to say.

"The good news is that the spinal cord is intact."

Before he could say another word, I interjected, "What? Why are you talking about his spinal cord? He just has some bad muscle spasms."

"No, Mrs. Walters, I'm afraid not. There is a subluxation of his first two vertebrae. Luckily, although they're dislocated, nothing has damaged the spinal cord."

The sterile hospital smell, mixed with this news, was making me nauseated. I grabbed Patrick's arm to steady me. All that was racing through my mind was, *This is a freak accident.* How many times do kids put their heads on the floor, or tumble, or wrestle?

My thoughts were interrupted by a nurse who entered the room as the doctor left and pronounced, "We really need to get him to a neurologist."

A neurologist? I really didn't know of any pediatric neurologists specifically, but I did know of several neurologists and neurosurgeons in the area because of my husband's previous brain tumor. Scrolling through the names in my head, I vaguely remembered that my husband's neurosurgeon also had pediatric experience. Before she could say anything else, I said, "I want him to see my husband's neurosurgeon. At one point he had been a pediatric neurosurgeon at another hospital."

The spunky nurse in her faded, well-worn scrubs appeared taken aback by my request but seemed to go along with it, for now. She left the room to call our neurosurgeon but came back only fifteen minutes later.

"I'm sorry. I called your doctor's office and he's on vacation."

The acid building from my anxiety crept up toward my throat. As she began to recommend another neurologist at a hospital nearby, I cut her off. I knew the neurologist she was mentioning, and he did not have pediatric experience.

"He is going to Children's Hospital or any pediatric hospital and will be seen and treated by a pediatric neurologist. He will not be going to just any other hospital with a small pediatric unit where he might be seen by just any neurologist."

The nurse's eyes narrowed, and she let out an audible sigh. "Ma'am, I don't think you understand. We need to transport your son *now*."

Standing, I looked directly at her and said, "No, I understand very well. And I don't think you understand. He's a kid, and children's bodies are different. I will not have him treated for a neurological issue by anyone other than a pediatric neurologist or neurosurgeon. You can make any statement that you want, but I refuse to grant you permission to transport my child to anything other than a pediatric hospital." Although I knew the clock was ticking for my son, I also knew from prior experience what can happen when a doctor lacking pediatric experience works with a child. I didn't want to take this chance with my Jordan, especially given the seriousness of his condition. I only hoped that pushing to be seen by the right kind of doctor didn't jeopardize the time sensitivity of the issue.

The nurse saw she was not getting anywhere. "If that is

what *you* really want, then I'll see what I can do." With that she pulled the curtain aside and stepped out.

Within two hours of her call to Children's Hospital, they told us that the helicopter was ready to go. We stood by as they prepped Jordan for travel. He was on morphine, with his head and body immobilized—taped to the board because they didn't want him to move. Helpless, I stared at my son, who was terrified and screaming, and there was nothing I could do to calm him.

There was nothing I could do to calm *me*.

Patrick tried to calm me, to reassure me and Jordan that everything was going to be all right. But knowing what I did about neck injuries, I wasn't so sure. I had only thought it was muscle spasms; it never would have occurred to me that Jordan could have done this much damage.

A moment later the helicopter transport crewman walked in and looked at Patrick and me. Before he pulled my son from me, I informed him that I was coming.

The transport crewman looked at me. "Ma'am, how much do you weigh?"

"One hundred pounds."

His eyes scanned my body. "No, you don't."

"What do you need me to weigh, because I need to be in *that* helicopter with my son." My unwavering arm was outstretched, pointing toward the door leading to the helicopter pad.

"Listen, ma'am, I am not going to jeopardize my crew because of your additional weight in my chopper."

My arm dropped to my side. Breaking down, I leveled with him, praying that I would not exceed their weight limit. "I weigh one hundred forty pounds."

The crewman nodded a curt approval. "You can come."

Patrick kissed us both good-bye, with assurances that he would meet us at the other hospital later. Then the crewman grabbed the side of Jordan's gurney and wheeled it toward the helicopter landing pad. Within seconds the helicopter landed and the crew inside it met us, the winds generated from the blades carrying their words away.

In the helicopter I held Jordan's hand and focused my eyes on his. I told him about all of the landmarks we were flying over. Anything to keep his attention focused on me, anything to lessen his fear. I don't know if it worked or not, but if it did, even in a small way, then at least I was doing *something* to help him.

After we arrived, we learned that the neurosurgeon was delayed. With each passing hour Jordan was losing patience with his immobility, the morphine not sedating him. To make a bad situation worse, the nurses insisted on putting a diaper on him. Jordan kept screaming, "I'm six. I don't need a diaper!" Looking at him, all I could think was, *Yes, you are six and you have no idea how serious this is.*

Right before they wheeled Jordan into the operating room to put the vertebrae back in place, Patrick and Peter arrived by car so that I wasn't alone. After a few hours the doctors came out.

"Mr. and Mrs. Walters, we have good news. We were able to realign Jordan's vertebrae without surgical intervention. However, he will need to wear a hard collar for the next three months." A smile radiated from the surgeon.

My eyes filled with the good news and Patrick hugged me, burying his head in my hair. We then turned to Peter—who obviously didn't understand the details but understood enough to know that it was good. We held him in our arms and I said a prayer that I wouldn't have to see the inside of a pediatric hospital ever again.

Jordan is nine now and is otherwise a normal child. Occasionally he complains of neck pain and we monitor things, but other than that he is normal. Would we have had the same outcome had he gone to a more general hospital? *Maybe.* Was I going to chance it? No.

If your child is seriously injured or has a serious medical condition, insist on a pediatric specialist in that area. Children's structures, bodies, and functions are very different from those of adults. Don't be afraid to push for what you know is best for your child.

Checkmate

*Doug's Missing Pages: When your child is
nothing like you and you can't connect*

WHEN I WAS GROWING UP, the only way I really bonded with my
father was through sports. From a very early age he coached me—
baseball mostly. But then again we watched everything together—
all sports, that is. For some reason, when my son Johnny was
born, I guess I figured it would be the same with him.

Don't get me wrong, I tried. Lord knows I tried. I tried
watching sports with him, but he wasn't interested. Then I tried
being his baseball coach, but that failed too. You go with what
you know, right? I tried to bond with Johnny the way my dad had
with me—through sports.

I grew up with sports, loving sports and playing or watching
sports in my free time. Either watching or playing, that's what I
do. Since Johnny has no interest in sports, I really didn't know

what to do with him. Sometimes I would joke with Marie that he must've gotten interests, like reading or music, from "your side of the family." I always made sure he wasn't around, because I never wanted him to feel I loved him less, but that was how I felt. How could this boy be mine and yet be so completely different from me? Growing up, and even now, I had always been considered a jock; I had no idea how to connect with my bookworm son.

One day when Johnny was about eleven years old, Marie and I were in the kitchen, talking about Johnny and how I couldn't really bond with him.

"Since nothing you enjoy really excites Johnny, and the things he likes don't interest you, why don't you find something that is new to both of you? Why don't you find something that you both can learn about *together*?"

On the surface it made sense. Nothing else had worked thus far.

"Do you have any thoughts on what we could do? What might interest both of us?"

"No, dear, I'm afraid you're gonna have to figure that one out on your own."

What on earth could we *both* want to learn together?

At first I didn't have any ideas, until I went into the basement and found some old cards that I had been given as a Christmas gift. They were chess cards where each card had a different move to make. You follow the cards until you learn how to play. Vaguely I recalled that there was one of those five-in-one game boards with chess pieces in it in the basement too. I had always wanted to learn how to play chess, so I figured why not?

It was a quiet winter Saturday when I dusted all the chess stuff off and brought it up. I called Johnny down and told him I wanted to talk to him. When he came into the living room and saw that the television was off and I was sitting there at a table with a chess set, he must've thought I'd lost my mind. He stood quietly in the doorway for a moment before he spoke.

"Uh, Dad, what did you, uh, want?"

"Well, I was, umm, thinking that we might learn to play chess. I don't know anything about it and neither do you, but I was thinking maybe we could figure it out together."

Shrugging his shoulders, Johnny said, "Sure, I guess."

Johnny sat down with me and we began to figure out the game of chess. Day after day we learned together how to play. Sometimes the game would last a few days, other times a few hours. Regardless, we used the time not only to play but to talk as well. I was slowly getting to know my son.

Finally we had something in common. It wasn't sports, but I realized it didn't have to be. Although it wasn't much, it was something, and it laid the foundation for a new kind of relationship. Now that we've mastered chess, we've decided to take on cribbage. After that it may be another game. Frankly, I don't care how many games I have learn how to play as long as I can keep doing it with my son and have moments to share with him.

Your child may be totally different from you, but everyone has something in common with someone in their life. Sometimes you just have to hunt harder to find it. It is about getting to know your child and finding ways to keep connected. Learn to accept your child for who they are, not who you think they should be.

Postpartum Depression Is Real

Sandy's Missing Pages: When you can't connect with your new baby

RUSS AND I WERE MARRIED in October and wanted to start a family right away. To our surprise, I got pregnant on our honeymoon. We were thrilled until we went for our eight-week appointment and they couldn't find a heartbeat. I had miscarried. Although we were sad, a part of us never thought I would get pregnant that quickly anyway. We accepted that perhaps it wasn't meant to be.

The doctor advised us to wait three months before trying to get pregnant again. We waited almost that long; it was the end of January when we found out I was pregnant for the second time. We were excited but tentative. After all, we had just been down this road and prayed we wouldn't lose this baby.

The pregnancy was great. I know many people who have horrible pregnancies, but I didn't. I was nauseated only in the afternoons through the second trimester, slept well, ate well, and really didn't gain much weight. It was easy overall and I was thrilled and excited to be a mom. The only stress that I had was constantly wondering if something was going to go wrong and that I might lose this baby too.

But I didn't. Everything went fine and the pregnancy was really uneventful. I went into labor in the middle of the night and had the baby naturally the next day. When we found out we had a boy, we were both really excited. We would have been happy with any healthy child, but because Russ is an only child, having a boy meant there would be someone to carry on his family name—something I knew was very important to him.

The first few days home we went through the motions: feeding, sleeping, diaper changes. That was when the problems began. The problems were not with our newborn son Dylan, however, but rather with me.

One morning, a week after I returned home from the hospital, I couldn't get out of bed. I knew I should get up, but I couldn't do it. It was time for Dylan to eat, but I wasn't looking forward to it. I heard him stirring in his bassinet. I propped myself up and looked at his tiny body. There he was, this beautiful little boy, a boy we had hoped and prayed for after the miscarriage—but something was missing. I was numb to him. So many of my friends had talked about instantly falling in love with their newborns, yet I felt nothing like that.

Lifting him to my body, I adjusted my bra and held him to me. He latched on and began to suck. After a few minutes he pulled away from me and started to cry. I turned the small bundle so that I was looking him in the face.

My own tears began to dot his yellow onesie. I kept searching his face for something to help me understand why I couldn't do this. He was my son; I should be able to figure this out, right? I couldn't find the answers, frustrated at my own inability to innately be a mom.

That day passed like many of the others. Eventually I gave up nursing, instead pumping and trying to give him my milk that way. Even that failed, forcing me to resort to bottles and formula. Still there was no peace.

My nights were sleepless. Not because of him, but because I began to have panic attacks. I would lie in bed at night and wonder about this and that, what tomorrow would bring and how I would manage his first birthday. I wasn't sleeping at night, which made the days that much worse. It got to a point where I couldn't get out of bed anymore. Thankfully my mother was with us, but even she didn't know what to do with me.

After a month of this, Russ came home one day from work to find me crying yet again. Once he greeted my mother and our son downstairs, he ventured up to where he knew he would find me. Yet again I couldn't get out of bed. Instead I was in my cocoon, curled up on my side crying.

"Sandy, why are you crying?"

Between sobs I managed a response. The words that I had known to be true since the day I saw Dylan for the first time spilled from me.

"I don't. Think. I. Can. Do. This."

"Do what, honey? I don't understand."

Grabbing a tissue, I blew my nose and tried to calm myself down.

"Russ, I don't think I can be a parent."

The look on his face indicated that he thought I was being ridiculous. I was known for being the Pied Piper of kids. I was great with my friends' kids, my nieces and nephews. Why wouldn't I make a great parent?

But I knew something that he didn't.

"You know how they say you're supposed to feel instantly in love with your child? Well, I don't feel that, Russ. I don't feel any of that. I don't have that maternal instinct that I've seen come out naturally with my friends. I know I should. Hell, I can't even nurse Dylan correctly. I don't think I can be a mom."

With that, my head dropped and I continued to cry. Russ sat there quietly looking at me, an expression of worry mixed with sadness painted across his face.

"Sandy, look, we'll go see the doctor about this."

Afraid I wouldn't be able to control the tears if I spoke, I nodded a quiet yes and pulled the covers over me a little tighter.

The day before the appointment, I sat watching an afternoon talk show, and they were doing a special on postpartum depression. As they talked about the guest and her story I began to realize how much we had in common, only this woman was in far worse shape than I was. It was the first time that I realized this might be something more than me just thinking I was an inadequate mother.

The next day we met with my obstetrician. Regardless of my good relationship with her, I found it hard to initially express my emotions. Taking a deep breath, I began with a few of the little things.

"The first few days home, I think we both went through the motions. I had a hard time adjusting but figured it was just part of the transition into becoming a new mother."

The doctor nodded and took a few notes down.

"But then within a week I could hardly get out of bed and spent the day crying on and off. It got worse from there, until I could barely get out of bed at all. I think the worst part about it is that I just don't feel an emotional connection to my son."

Russ glanced at me and squeezed my hand, offering little but much-needed support.

I went on to detail the sleepless nights and panic attacks, the isolation of being trapped in my home—basically everything that I had been experiencing over the last month. Wrapping it up, I began to cry.

"I miss my old life. I don't know why I thought I could be a mother."

"Sandy, you have the classic signs of postpartum depression. Everything that you are experiencing is normal, and it doesn't mean that you were never meant to be a mom. The missing-your-old-life part is normal, and it's also common with postpartum. Would you be open to trying an antidepressant for a little bit?"

"Yeah, I'd be open to it." At that point, I'd have been open to just about any suggestion the doctor had.

"Also, I'd recommend trying to get out of the house more. See your friends as you used to. You may find that it also boosts your spirits and helps make you feel more like your old self."

Thanking the doctor for her time, we left her office with a Lexapro prescription in hand and immediately went to the pharmacy to get it filled. If this was going to help, I wanted to get started right away rather than wait any longer.

When we arrived home, my mother greeted me at the door. Having lived with us over the last month caring for Dylan—especially on the days when I couldn't even care for him—she had witnessed my struggle with depression firsthand and knew how scared I was that I didn't feel an emotional bond yet with my son. Holding Dylan in her arms, she handed him to me and said, "You're going to look at this boy one day and be so in love with him, you won't know what to do with yourself."

All I said in return was, "I hope so, Mom."

In the month following that appointment, the medication had fully kicked in and I slowly learned to celebrate the small accomplishments in parenting. If I managed to soothe Dylan, I would view that as one thing I had done *right*. With each passing day I added another accomplishment and realized soon enough that there were many things I was doing right as a parent but not giving myself credit for. As I became stronger, I was able to enjoy my son more, and I was finally able to begin to really develop that bond with him. By the time Dylan turned three months old, I finally felt good and no longer needed the medication.

I only wish that people talked about postpartum depression more openly. As I went through my experience with postpartum depression, I began talking about it to other moms I knew and learned more about it. What I realized is that despite how normal postpartum depression actually is, many people go through it and don't say anything or get help because they are afraid that there is something wrong with them. Unfortunately their guilt, and the need to hide their feelings, further fuels the depression and the cycle repeats.

Pay attention to your feelings. If necessary, go talk to your doctor and get help. Don't waste precious time not enjoying your baby, because you can't get those moments back.

Breaking All the Rules

Emily's Missing Pages: When your current discipline methods aren't working

THE GIRLS WERE SEATED at either end of the kitchen table, the length of which was acting as a much-needed barrier between them. Their faces were set in contorted smirks, their arms crossed. I bent down to pick up a toy and out of the corner of my eye I saw Maya turn toward Annabelle and stick her tongue out.

"Moooooommmm!" Annabelle wailed.

"Maya, that's enough! You're nine years old; you know you can't treat your sister like this!"

"What? I didn't do anything! SHE started it!" Maya yelled, her arm outstretched pointing toward ten-year-old Annabelle, who was sitting at the other end of the table.

Maya's angry yell rang through the kitchen. The intensity and abruptness caused Cade, my two-year-old, to pause, albeit briefly, and stare at his two older sisters. My third daughter, Cameron, sat quietly reading in the family room chair. But I saw that she too was watching and waiting to see what was going to happen next.

Instead of addressing them, I picked up the remaining dinner dishes, turned, and put them on the counter. At eye level, taped to our kitchen cabinet doors, were our Family Rules. Rule number twenty: *No Fighting.* So much for that rule. The desire to leave them, this mess, raged. I wouldn't look at them. I couldn't. I didn't want them to see my disgust. It wasn't merely loathing their constant bickering; I was angered by my inability to be a better parent.

Finally I turned and broke the silence.

"Maya. Annabelle. Up to your rooms. Get ready for bed." The girls' mouths hung open, but before they managed say anything else, I stopped them.

"Mommy's done. I can't stand any more of this arguing. You're both going to bed, and if you don't want to lose pool time this weekend, you will listen." Infuriated and on the verge of tears, I wasn't sure how much more of this I could take. It was only early June, and if something didn't change soon I didn't know how we would all survive the summer.

Resigned, Annabelle got up from the table and walked away. Maya followed behind her, her exaggerated footsteps heavy on the wooden stairs.

"Cameron, I am going to bathe Cade. You can stay up until after I finish with him. Okay?" My dear six-year-old smiled a gentle smile beneath her soft brown eyes. I couldn't have been more thankful for that smile, and her usually good behavior.

Later that evening after everyone was in bed, I looked in at them. Each lay peacefully sleeping as if the day's drama and fighting had been completely washed from their memories. As is my nightly ritual, I adjusted their covers and kissed their foreheads.

I couldn't understand how it was possible to love my children as much as I did and equally not want to be around them.

Entering my room, I passed my night table, stacked a foot deep in parenting books. I had read them all. Unbelievably I was no closer at figuring out how to manage my two older girls. Exhausted, I didn't want to wash my face, brush my teeth, or do anything that I knew I was supposed to do. Instead, the bed called to me and I collapsed into it.

"Em? You okay?" Scott, my husband, said as he came into the room.

Turning my body, still lying down, I propped my head up with my arm and looked at him.

"Emily, what's going on?" Scott asked again while loosening his tie.

He really had no idea. While he had been out at a dinner meeting, he had completely missed World War Three in our household—a war that wouldn't have been complete without food being dumped "accidentally" by one sister onto the other.

"Scotty, I just don't know how I can continue. I don't want to hate our children, but something has got to give. I can't stand to be around them sometimes, or even look at them. And then tonight I kiss them while they are sleeping and wonder how it is that I can love and despise them so much at the same time. And it's not just them. They make me so incredibly mad, I'm not myself anymore. If I were our kids, I wouldn't want to be around me. I don't want their childhood memories of me being like this."

"Was it all of the kids or only Annabelle and Maya?"

"As usual, it was Annabelle and Maya—but everything they do affects *all* the kids."

Ever the optimist, my husband merely said, "I really don't think it's that bad. You'll figure it out."

Right. I'll figure it out. I'd made my way through a stack of books and still hadn't figured it out. If I had, I wouldn't be sitting here like this. Deflated, I slid my arm out from beneath my head, closed my eyes, and shut the world out.

The following morning I woke before the children and sneaked quietly down the hall to the kitchen. As the sun streamed in and reflected off our copper kitchen table, I sat there with my books and a notepad. It was like I was in college all over again, only unlike college, I was actually studying—studying how to be a parent.

What wasn't working and why? We had our rules, but the older two especially didn't seem to care about them or pay attention to them. How do you devise a consistent set of rules and means of enforcement for such a wide array of ages?

Annabelle was ten, Maya nine, Cameron six, and Cade two years old. The older ones were too old to be in time-outs. They simply didn't care anymore. Cameron was usually well behaved, but like any kid she occasionally had issues, so I needed something that could work for her as well. Then there was Cade; he was too young for much right now, but I wanted to find something that I could apply to all of the kids—in some form.

Managing the day-to-day with four kids is exhausting. Whatever I came up with would not only need to be adaptable for a variety of ages, it would also need to be easy to implement and enforce. If it wasn't, I wouldn't be able to follow through with it. Without enforcement, I knew there was no way anything was going to change.

The two older girls didn't behave like this elsewhere. Although school was now out for the year, there had never been any behavioral issues there. Why should they behave like this at home? Our home had become a battle zone. Annabelle and Maya would fight, sometimes involving Cameron. I'd go to battle with them and Cade would get upset. No one was winning; it had to stop.

I looked back at the set of rules the three girls and I had devised at the beginning of last spring. There had been behavior issues in which the three older kids were having trouble doing the right thing. In response, over spring break I sat down with them and devised these rules. When we did it, they seemed engaged and enthused to help create a solution. I thought that maybe this would work because it was a good set of rules. Unfortunately, for whatever reason they didn't seem interested or invested in them anymore.

One of the parenting books talked about a program using a behavior chart with stickers. Scanning it, I found some elements that I liked, but what I didn't like was rewarding kids for doing what they should be doing anyway. What do you do if the child misbehaves? Just give them a sad face sticker? It hardly seemed that that would be enough for *my* kids.

The sound of small feet on the stairs broke my concentration. It was time to pack things up, at least for now. I was not giving up on finding a resolution.

Throughout the next week I read more of the books and researched various websites. Many techniques that I had tried previously had not worked. Each time I followed the approaches or programs described to the letter. Now I wondered if that wasn't part of my problem. I needed to develop something that was perhaps tailored a bit to our family, a hybrid discipline approach. I wanted something easy and something tangible. With that goal in mind I developed our new ticket system.

My ticket system is based on others out there. It is a discipline system in which the child accumulates tickets or loses tickets based on behavior. The basis for losing a ticket was the set of rules that the children had already developed. A child who went above and beyond and did something without being asked would gain a ticket. Depending on the total number of tickets remaining at the end of the week, the child would either get a reward, lose a privilege, or neither.

I created a whole series of tickets out of paper, which I laminated and cut out. The tickets would be placed in the children's individually labeled plastic bags, which I hung on the inside of our kitchen cabinet. This way they could easily go in and see how many tickets they had on any given day. To make sure that Scott and I were on the same page with this, we met and discussed the overall strategy and how it would play out. Once we were in agreement, it was time to sit the kids down.

Scott and I arranged ourselves at the table with our four children. Each of them looked at me, wondering what was going to come next. It had been another rough week and we didn't often call family meetings.

"Guys, Daddy and I have been talking and we are really unhappy with how people have been behaving and getting along. No one seems to follow the rules. These rules were developed by us as a family, and they need to be followed as a family. Starting today, and each Sunday from now on, you will each receive seven tickets. If you break one of the rules, you will lose a ticket. If you drop below seven tickets by the time you go to bed on Saturday night, you will lose a privilege for the rest of the next week."

Annabelle and Maya looked at each other; Cameron looked at them, and then their eyes darted to Scott and then to me. Was it shock? Probably.

Maya was the first to speak up. "Mom! That's not fair!"

"Maya, what do you think is fair? Is it fair that you and Annabelle constantly fight and Cameron and Cade have to watch it? Is it fair that Mommy has to spend a lot of her time putting everyone in time-outs because no one can seem to follow the rules?"

Annabelle was next. "But, Mom, what if we accidentally break a rule? We'll be doomed for the whole next week!"

At this point Scott stepped in. "Guys, you do have the opportunity to *earn* tickets, so you aren't necessarily *doomed*," he said, with the same dramatic flair and inflection that Annabelle had used.

Clarifying, I added, "If you do something on your own to help out, or help each other, you can earn a ticket. Whatever it is can't be part of your normal chores, but something above and beyond that." Their little shoulders relaxed a bit, some of the anxiety removed.

Now it was time to reveal the last piece. Scott looked at me, and I continued my explanation.

"And . . . if you earn ten or more tickets you will get a prize. This could be a privilege, or an actual prize, but either Daddy or I get to decide." The excited looks passed from Annabelle to Maya and then down to Cameron. Cade still really didn't understand what was going on, but if this worked, he would understand someday.

The next month was better than I ever could have hoped for. There were weeks where the girls lost a privilege, like playing with friends or TV or computer time. Once they did, however, they did not seem to want to repeat the experience. Each of the kids also looked for new ways to help out around the house and sought out ways that they could assist each other, all in an effort to either maintain their seven tickets and avoid losing a privilege or because they wanted to earn enough for a prize.

Every family is different, and one size does not always fit all. It took some time, but with a little tweaking I was able to develop something that worked well for my family. For me, the tickets took some of the emotion out of disciplining. What I gained instead was a feeling of control. If there is a violation, I simply note it to my child and take away a ticket. I don't get as upset or frustrated anymore, which ultimately has led to a saner, healthier environment for my children and me.

For my children, this system allows them to really *own* their behavior. Let's face it, many days kids have discipline issues and will lose tickets. But giving them an opportunity to earn tickets back empowers them to make their own positive behavioral choices. The results they get at the end of the week, good or bad, are theirs and theirs alone—which I think is a great life lesson.

Sometimes when it comes to disciplining your children, it's important to make them feel empowered. With a little customization and creativity you can find what works best for your family.

Will Do Anything for a Lost Retainer

Mandy's Missing Pages: When you need to put aside your frustrations to help your child fix their own problem

THE BALMY AUGUST NIGHT was perfect for a good movie. The question was, which one? With my nine-year-old son, Shawn, and eight-year-old daughter, Brandi, we have found that their tastes sometimes do not quite mesh.

Brandi stood with her hands on her hips, "I don't want to go see some lame 'boy' comic movie, Mom! I want to go see *Madagascar 3*."

"*Mommmmm!* I don't want to go see a 'baby' movie," Shawn snapped back.

Frank's eyes met mine. Our children obviously were not going to agree. But maybe the solution was just that easy.

"Guys, what if we split up? I will take Brandi to see *Madagascar 3*, and Shawn, you and Daddy can go see *The Avengers*. We'll have to make sure that they're showing around the same time, but I think this should work. What do you say, guys?"

My two children looked at each other. Although they were getting what they wanted, no one had actually *won*, so I don't think they knew how to respond. Eventually they scattered to find their shoes and get ready to go.

A few minutes later, I stood in front of the door leading to the garage. As the children rounded the bend to the adjoining mud room I prevented them from racing out to the car. There was one more thing that needed to be addressed.

"Shawn."

"Yeah, Mom?"

"Are you planning on eating in the theater?"

"Yeah. Why?"

Scanning his body, I gratefully saw him wearing his khaki cargo shorts.

"Where do you think you should put your retainer while you're eating?"

Shawn initially responded with somewhat of a blank stare. Somehow the fact that the little piece of plastic in his mouth cost well over a thousand dollars hadn't really sunk in. I guess the look in my eyes, however, did because he followed them to the pocket I was staring at in his cargo shorts.

"Uh, I guess my shorts pocket?"

"Yup. That's your best bet for keeping it safe and not losing it."

I shot Frank a don't-forget-to-remind-him look, and we all made our way to the car and the movie theater.

Before we parted ways at the theater, I reminded both Frank and Shawn, "Don't forget to put your retainer in your pocket!" Eager to get into the popcorn line, they both nodded to acknowledge me and were soon ensconced in the world of the jumbo popcorn, Cokes, and Raisinets.

Madagascar 3 let out a little early, so we waited patiently for the boys to depart *The Avengers*. As soon as we saw Frank and Shawn they began regaling us with highlights from the movie. Their animated conversation distracted me so much that I didn't even think to ask about the retainer—that is, until we arrived back home.

As the kids went up to get ready for bed, I let Willy, our standard black poodle, out. After he was back in, I went up to tuck both of the kids to bed. I breezed in and out of Brandi's room first. But by the time I had gotten in there, she was already half asleep. Sitting on the edge of Shawn's bed, I turned to him.

"Hey, buddy. Don't forget to put your retainer back in."

In return, I saw panic rise in his eye. The red comforter thrown back, Shawn ran over to the hamper, frantically seeking out his cargo shorts. I watched as he held them up and patted down each pocket. Nothing. Not giving up yet, he put his hand in each one. By the time he reached the last pocket, his shoulders sagged. His eyes were filling up with tears.

This could mean only one thing: the retainer was gone.

"Shawn, where's your retainer? I thought you put it into your pocket?"

His head hung sheepishly low. "I think I might have put it in my lap, Mom. It must have fallen out of it."

The bill for the retainer flashed through my mind. And instead of sitting in Shawn's mouth, it was probably stuck to goo on the movie theater floor. I looked at my watch; it was after ten p.m. They would be in the middle of the later show; as a result, our search for the retainer would have to wait until the following morning.

Leaving him in bed, I went downstairs and broke the news to Frank. The retainer was lost, probably somewhere in Theater 15.

I was irritated that such an expensive item was carelessly taken out and that all attempts to remind Shawn to take care of it were ignored. The question was, how do we handle this? Do we express our anger and make him feel guilty for losing it, or do we focus on the solution? Thinking of Shawn's panicked face when I tucked him in, I was pretty sure he felt guilty enough. No, harping on this was not going to be productive.

"Well, what do you think we should do? Despite being lost, it is probably disgusting at this point. Should we even bother to look for it?"

Frank studied his hands and then me. "Well, if we find it we can see if it can be salvaged. I do think he should go look for it. I mean, that thing cost a fortune! I'll take him back there tomorrow morning. After all, I should have made sure he put it safely away."

The same thoughts had crossed my mind, so I was glad that we were in agreement. However, I did not envy the two of them crawling around on the floor looking for it. Visions of them inching through the spilled soda and crushed popcorn filled my mind. I imagined Shawn's retainer stuck to the floor, held in place by high fructose corn syrup.

The next morning Shawn came downstairs to breakfast. He swirled the cereal squares around in the milk, occasionally taking a bite. Before long he pushed it away and looked up at me.

"Mom, I'm so, so, so sorry. You told me and reminded me and I forgot."

Frank entered the room, and while pouring himself coffee he added, "You know, I forgot too, kiddo. We both forgot."

I was angry—angry at both of them—but last night I'd realized that being angry or yelling or flipping out wasn't going to be productive.

"I know you're sorry, Shawn. It's upsetting because that retainer, as you know, is really expensive. But before we look into replacing it, you and Dad are going back to the theater to look for it. Who knows, maybe you can find it."

"Maybe we will, Mom!" Shawn said, his face lit with hope.

Right after breakfast, Frank and Shawn drove to the theater and embarked on the grand search. When they first got there, they met with the manager and explained when and where the retainer had been lost. Back in Theater 15, Frank and Shawn found the lights dimmed. Even though no movie was playing, the lights were set at a lower setting.

The thought of bringing a flashlight had never occurred to anyone. Not only were they going to have to search the theater, they were going to have to do it in the dark.

For the next fifteen minutes the two hunted between the rows. Using their hands to navigate the floor and the mysterious things that lay on it in the dimly lit theater, they hoped that somehow they would find the retainer. Thankfully—sort of—the theater staff had done a less-than-stellar job of cleaning up from the night before; consequently, a lot was still left on the floor, which meant there was a pretty good chance the retainer was still there. However, it also meant that there was a lot of debris that had to be sorted through if it was going to be found.

Row after row, seat after seat, they searched until Shawn's hand reached something that felt like his retainer. It was stuck in a pool of soda goo. Pulling it up from the floor, he yelled out, "Daaaaad! I found it!"

Shawn looked at his hand, wrinkled his nose, and said, "This is so gross!"

As soon as they returned home and walked through the door, Shawn outstretched his sticky hands to reveal the retainer. Gingerly I lifted it from one of his palms and instructed him to go to the bathroom and wash his hands a few times. Holding the retainer, I really wasn't sure what to do next. Putting it into a plastic container on the counter, I went to the kitchen sink to wash my own hands. The retainer was disgustingly filthy, and I couldn't imagine how I was going to get it clean enough to put back in my son's mouth.

Wiping my hands on a towel, I sat down at the kitchen table, turned on my laptop, and began to search the Internet for answers. Normally I would think to boil it, but I thought that might not be a good idea because it might melt and lose its shape. After being lucky enough to find it, I'd hate now to do the wrong thing and ruin it, all in desperate attempts to sterilize it from the theater muck.

Other sites listed a variety of approaches, and finally I settled on my own protocol. First I washed it several times with soap, hot water, and an old toothbrush. Then it was on to soaking in a cleaner called Retainer Brite. Last but not least, I contacted a close friend who was a dentist and asked if they could sterilize it for me. We went to their offices, where it was soaked in a denture sterilization solution for an hour.

Before handing Shawn back his retainer, I wanted to make sure he was clear that this should never happen again.

"Next time . . ." I waited until I had Shawn's full attention. "Next time, you want to take your retainer out you need to put it directly into its case. If you don't have a case, use a baggie or something. It's too easy to wrap it up in a paper towel or napkin and forget about it. Okay?"

"Oh, I *know*, Mom. Trust me, I never want to have to look for that retainer again!"

With the retainer safely returned to Shawn's mouth, I smiled. I was glad he was able to find it but also glad he had been actively involved in fixing his own problem. We could have gotten angry, punished him, and simply replaced it, but I think the way it worked out provided a much stronger lesson to our son.

*In every situation we have a choice to perpetuate
blame or turn the situation into something positive.
Sometimes, saying little and supporting a child in resolving
their own mistake will have a larger impact than harping
on the issue.*

Am I Gay?

*Alicia's Missing Pages: When a child feels
pressured to define her sexuality*

MY DAUGHTER WHITNEY entered the ninth grade a few weeks after her fourteenth birthday. Whitney immersed herself in a host of activities but loved soccer and the school newspaper the best. Being in high school opened a new world for Whitney, one of new friends, sports, and social activities. So much so, she really didn't seem to pay much attention to boys. Occasionally she mentioned how cute one was, but overall, they simply didn't appear to be on her radar screen.

As the fall progressed she began to get more and more involved with soccer and began to hang out with some of the upper-class girls; one of these, named Olivia, began spending a lot of time with Whitney. At first I was excited that someone had taken her under her wing, but later I began to notice little things. Initially it was a bracelet that I'd never seen on Whitney. Then one day she came home from soccer wearing a knit ski cap that I knew wasn't hers. When I questioned her on it, her response was, "Oh, it was cold out, so Olivia gave it to me. She said I could keep it."

At first it all seemed reasonable, but as time went on other things began appearing. Hanging up Whitney's clothes in her closet, I began to notice new shirts and sweaters appearing. I knew that teenage girls shared clothes, but these weren't items being shared. Instead my daughter told me that they were more gifts from Olivia. Although I was glad she was making new friends, I found it strange that a new friend would be showering her with trinkets and clothing.

Then there were the subtle behavior changes. One morning I had made her favorite breakfast—a western omelet with extra cheese, bacon, and orange juice. Instead of being excited to see it, as she normally would be, Whitney merely poked at it and then told me all the reasons why we shouldn't eat eggs, dairy, or bacon. This sudden change in her tastes seemed out of left field and left me perplexed. When I asked her where she'd heard all of this, I was met with, "Olivia told me. In fact she said I should *never* eat those things. So I've stopped." It all seemed very strange and out of character for my daughter.

The end of October approached and I came into the kitchen to make a cup of afternoon tea. The last traces of sunlight were fading; darkness was coming earlier. Whitney sat at the table, oblivious to her math homework. Twirling her well-worn pencil between her fingers, she made small gray circles on her thumb. Her faraway look triggered my mom radar; something wasn't right—something was definitely off.

"Whitney, would you like a cup of tea or something? Dinner won't be ready for another hour."

She didn't look up from her pencil; instead she twirled it over and over again between her fingers.

"Whitney? Did you hear me?"

Seemingly startled, she raised her head, turning it in my direction. "What?"

"Darling, is something bothering you?"

Whitney averted her gaze from me. The twirling of the pencil continued. And then she said, "Mom, do you think women's bodies are beautiful?"

Thinking maybe this was a self-esteem or body-image issue, I answered, "Yes, honey, I think women's bodies are beautiful. They have been depicted in paintings for centuries. Why on earth are you asking?"

"Olivia asked, and I told her I thought they were beautiful. She said that if I felt that way, it was a sign I was gay, that I liked girls. But I just don't know, Mom."

I really didn't know how to handle this. I put my mug of tea on the table and tried to gather myself. Over the fall she really hadn't talked much about boys, except for one—Nathan. He was a young man in her science class with whom she'd done a project. Whitney had told me she thought he was cute but out of her league. She definitely had some passing interest in him. The truth was she was young, and given her life experience and age, I wondered if she really had any idea of where her sexual orientation lay. True, she did have some boy friends who had already come out, but everyone develops on a different time-table. I knew whatever I said next needed to be supportive and neutral. She was trying to figure herself out, and I wanted to make sure she had the freedom and space to do so—without judgment.

"At this time in your life, your body is going through a lot of changes. You're figuring out what you like and don't like, and who you are and are not attracted to. This is all normal.

Some people know very early on what their sexual orientation is; in others it takes a little longer. No one develops at the same rate, and that's okay. But just because you think a woman's body is beautiful doesn't mean that you are a lesbian or even bisexual. Does that make sense, honey?"

The offhand nod Whitney returned indicated she was finished opening up with me on this subject for now. This was not a closed subject; Whitney was bound to have more questions. I knew I needed to have the lines of communication open, and I wanted her to be comfortable continuing to talk to me.

Over the next few weeks I noticed more trinkets appearing, all from Olivia. While doing laundry, I went through Whitney's jeans pockets as I normally do before putting them in the laundry. Only this day, I found a few notes from Olivia to Whitney. The notes were intense. In them Olivia urged Whitney to make a decision, that if she really cared for Olivia she would. From what I gathered it looked like Olivia wanted Whitney to make a decision about her sexual orientation. It concerned me that anyone would be pressuring my daughter to define her sexuality. It was time for another talk.

Friday afternoon, after she came home from school, I pulled Whitney into the kitchen. I wanted to talk to her before the weekend came and she was consumed with social activities.

Tentatively Whitney slid into the ladder-back kitchen chair. Her hands were clasped together; she eyed me with guarded anticipation. "Okay. What's up, Mom?"

Taking a deep breath, I began questioning her about the notes, about Olivia, about the last few weeks. What emerged was that Olivia, at nearly seventeen, had already defined who she was sexually. She had developed a crush on Whitney and was pressuring her to define her own sexuality. What also unfolded was really how confused my daughter was. She would talk about how cute Nathan was and wondered if she might run into him at the movies that weekend, and then in the next moment talk about how much she cared about Olivia.

However, the thing that concerned me the most was her response when I asked if she had told Olivia about her feelings about Nathan and her confusion. I asked Whitney if she had made it clear to Olivia that she was only beginning to figure this all out. Her response: "Olivia made it clear that if I didn't choose her, our friendship was over. She's my friend, Mom; I don't want to lose her."

Here was my young daughter trying to develop her identity while being showered with attention from an upperclassman. The attention had enabled her to start to come out of her shell, but as a consequence of that attention, she was being pressured to define her sexuality—well before she was ready to do so.

It seemed like only yesterday that I was braiding Whitney's hair in pigtails and her biggest concern was over what play date she was going to have. Now I felt she was being manipulated by someone who she thought was her friend—and it infuriated me. I wanted my daughter to be able to grow and discover herself on her own timetable, not someone else's.

"Whitney, I think you need to set some boundaries with Olivia. I know she is your friend and you've had a lot of fun, but frankly, you're really young. This is *your* time to discover who *you* are. Sweetie, just tell Olivia how much you care about her, but you aren't ready to make any decisions yet . . . that you are just trying to figure it out. And . . . I hate to say this, but maybe you shouldn't hang out with her as much right now. No true friend would pressure another to do anything they weren't ready to do."

Whitney once again nodded, her eyes brimming with tears. Clearly this had been weighing heavily on her.

"All right, Mom," she said in a whisper, and slid out of the chair and away from me.

Up until now I'd figured it was something that would pass; I had no real idea of the magnitude of Olivia's feelings for my daughter. Given the depth of what was unfolding, it was time for me to discuss this with my husband, Dominic.

Sitting down with Dominic was not easy. Dominic lived in a very black-and-white world—there were no shades of gray. Right now, our daughter was a shade of gray. I could only hope that he would understand and not jump to anything rash. What we were both clear on was our genuine concern that undue pressure was being exerted on our daughter to determine her sexual orientation before she was ready. Peer pressure from anyone, boy or girl, was not okay with us.

From Thanksgiving to Christmas, things appeared to have abated, at least on the surface. There were no new gifts, no new notes. Whitney began to hang out with some other classmates: going shopping, to the movies, or over to other friend's houses. When I asked Whitney about school or her friends, she was a typical noncommittal teenager. She seemed to be adjusting to high school well and also appeared less troubled or distracted than she had been in the fall. There were no outward signs of a possible problem until right before Christmas.

Whitney came home from school ready for Christmas break. Dropping her bag in the kitchen, she continued on toward the living room. Right as I was about to walk into the living room, I saw her nestled in the couch, holding something in her hands, a bracelet. I stopped and watched from the doorway as she alternatively studied it and looked out of the window. I had a pretty good guess as to whom it was from and why my daughter had a pensive look on her face.

"Whitney?"

Startled, Whitney tried to casually slip the bracelet between two cushions.

"Who's that from?"

My question prompted Whitney to retrieve the bracelet from the cushions. Her eyes confirmed my suspicions before she said another word.

Sliding down next to her, her toes touching the edge of my thigh, I reached out and put my hand on her shin.

"Sweetie, what's bothering you? I thought you had talked to Olivia, that things had gotten better?"

"I did, Mom. But she still wants me to make a choice. She says she loves me. She's my closest friend. I don't want to lose her, but I don't know that I care about her the way she cares about me. I don't know, and I'm so confused! How can I feel so close but not be ready to choose at the same time?" Whitney's head dropped and the sobs came.

This was too much. My daughter needed the time to figure herself out, free from external pressures. It was time for some parental intervention.

That evening, with Whitney out of earshot, I discussed the issue with Dominic. We both agreed that something needed to be done because this young woman was not respecting our daughter's boundaries. The next day Dominic made a visit to the girl's home and asked to speak with her parents. In the discussion he explained what had transpired over the last few months; he asked that they speak with their daughter about leaving Whitney alone for a little bit. Obviously what was developing was not a healthy relationship for either of them. Time would tell whether their relationship could or would continue, but in the interim Whitney needed less stress.

After the talk with Olivia's parents, the pressure on Whitney abated. As it did, and she spent more time with people other than just Olivia, Whitney developed new circles of friends. It was as if a weight was lifted from Whitney and she could finally have the time and space to figure out who she was.

As parents we need to support, and at times defend, our children's right to adequate time and space to figure out their sexuality. Every child develops at their own rate and no one should ever be pressured to prematurely define who they are.

Put Me In, Coach,
I'm Ready to Play

*Brian's Missing Pages: When your child's sports team
becomes embroiled in adult politics*

AT EIGHT YEARS OLD, my son Tim was obsessed with baseball.
He wanted to play it year round. He collected baseball cards and
even had a shrine to his favorite local team in his bedroom. It was
no surprise to frequently hear baseball talk tossed about between
Tim and his friends. One Thursday, as I filled in for my wife
in the car pool, the boys in the backseat of our Chevy Suburban
turned the conversation to baseball once again.

"Hey Tim, did you know they are splittin' up our team and
puttin' the younger guys on another team—you know, like my
brother, who has never played?" Tim's friend Brady said.

"Well . . . I guess that makes sense to put us 'big guys'
together. I mean we've been playin' together for a long time,"

Tim said. While he nodded emphatically, I sensed him looking at me.

Our eyes met in the rearview mirror. Tim wanted assurance that he was still going to be with his friends. The fact that his friend Brady had all of this information was suspect, but at the moment all I did was smile in return and make a mental note to investigate further.

Over the next few days the full picture emerged. Of ten eight- to nine-year-olds, seven children were moved up to a better team and three of the older children, including my son, were pushed down to a team made up primarily of six-year-olds. It was a creation of a team where the best players, and the coaches' sons, were moved and the less-desired players discarded.

The new team was composed of mostly older children and was called a "kid-pitch" team. Based on the ages of the children on the original team, this was what they would have morphed into during the spring season anyway. However, the coaches' decision to prematurely pull some of the players up to an existing fall kid-pitch team not only fractured the existing team but also further divided the skill sets of the children—so much so that even if the original team of players rejoined in the spring, the experience and cohesion of the advanced players would most likely set them apart from the kids who were left behind, alienating the less-skilled teammates. I couldn't explain the logic, except that adult politics and egos appeared to be infiltrating even the youngest levels on what was supposed to be a noncompetitive, recreational team. From the outside looking in, it looked as if this quite possibly had been done to create a "winning" team.

For my son, I needed to figure out what to do next. Tim knew he wasn't as good as the other players. However, it would humiliate him if he were relegated to a younger team, playing with Brady's younger brother while his best friend, Brady, watched. In addition, I was concerned that he would stagnate at the lower level and not continue to grow and develop. It was time to think outside the box.

I approached my neighbor Eric, who had been a coach previously, and discussed the situation. He knew Tim well, knew his skill set, and his own son had been one of the players moved up. Eric suggested approaching the coach with an alternative approach. Perhaps there would be a way to allow Tim to be on the team and practice with them, but with the understanding that because his skills were on the lower end, perhaps he might not get as much playing time. Although it wasn't ideal, it would allow Tim to move with his friends and, more important, allow him to continue to grow and develop his skill set. But before speaking with the coach, I really needed to sit down with my son, break the bad news and see if he would be interested in even doing what I was about to propose.

After dinner, my wife took our daughter down to our playset and I sat to talk with Tim.

"Hey, buddy, I heard from Coach Jack about fall ball."

"Yeah? When do practices start? I'm going to be really good at fielding this year, Dad, you know? I've been practicing a lot with the bounceback. I'm goin' to knock their socks off." He looked at me with an optimistic grin. Tim was excited, which was why what I had to say next was so hard.

"Tim. That's the thing. They've decided to break the team up. You're supposed to go back to Coach Adam's team instead of to Coach Jack's team."

Tim's eyes filled up. He looked away from me so I wouldn't see the tears falling down his cheeks. Wiping them away with his hand, he turned to face me.

"Why, Dad? Why did they put me on the little guys' team?"

"Bud, they took some of the better players and put them on a kid-pitch team. They were concerned it might be too advanced for you." I then rattled off the names of the kids who were advancing, and soon Tim moved to the next obvious question.

"But, Dad, some of those players are exactly like me. We've got the same stats! How come they got to move and I didn't?"

Ah, now an important lesson about life and politics.

"Yeah, I know, Tim. But those kids are all the coaches' sons. They get included because their dads help coach the team."

"But that's not fair!"

"I know, buddy, but that's just how life works sometimes. But listen, I was thinking maybe we could ask Coach Jack if you could still be on the team, practice with them and stuff. The only catch would be, since you are a younger player, you might not get as much game time. You would have to work harder than some of the other kids and practice more to prove to the coaches that you're ready for more time on the field. Would you want to try that, or would you rather go to Coach Adam's team?"

For the first time since we began the conversation, I saw a gleam of hope in Tim's eyes.

"I don't care if I don't get to play as much, Dad; I just want to learn and get better and play with my friends." Then he said what I knew was coming next. "I can't play on Coach Adam's team. I can't be on that team with Brady's younger brother and have Brady come to my games to watch me."

Now it was time to see if we might be able to get it worked out with Coach Jack. I had my doubts about whether it would work, and whether I even wanted it to work. Having my son on a team where he wasn't wanted was not the most ideal situation and could be fraught with problems. But I knew that Tim wanted to try, and I wanted to support him.

Over the next several days, Jack and I exchanged a slew of e-mails. Initially we were told it might work, that Tim would be wait-listed on the kid-pitch team. Each day, Tim asked if he was going to get to play with his coach, his team. In response, we tried to be noncommittal and prepared alternative options for him should it not come to fruition.

Finally, a week later there was a reversal. The reversal came with an explanation that given Tim's age relative to the other kids, he should be on a lower team. This was clearly another way to push him out, even though he actually was one of the oldest of his age group on the team—a point we made to the baseball commissioner when we notified him that we were not returning that fall.

When we finally broke the news to Tim, he was upset, but enough time had passed that he had begun to look forward to the alternatives. Ultimately he decided to play on a similar team in a different league. This team focused on really preparing the kids for the next level, and the league seemed more intent on making sure that the kids had fun and learned strong skills, rather than stacking a winning team. The coaches in the new league made it known from the beginning that winning and the score were not as important as trying your hardest and developing your skill. In the end, it turned out to be a much healthier environment for my son—and one that was free from adult goals and politics.

As parents, we have a responsibility to thoroughly investigate youth sport leagues and coaches, just as we would schools, teachers, or caregivers. Make sure that the sports environment that you are exposing your kid to is as free as possible from adult goals and agendas. Doing so will help preserve the fun and skill development in younger children's sports programs.

We've Created a Monster

*Kate's Missing Pages: When poor parenting choices
make it hard to correct bad behavior*

WHEN I WAS A CHILD, my family struggled financially. As a parent I wanted to do everything within my power to provide well for my child and make sure that she had financial security and stability and hopefully one day could go to college and not worry about student loans.

Before my husband, Vince, and I had children, we discussed how we would parent and whether I would return to work. My love for my job and the desire to provide amply for my child resulted in the decision that I would return to work. What we didn't anticipate was how difficult it would be not to have as much time with Allison as we would like.

After we got off work, we each took turns picking Allison up from the daycare a few blocks from our apartment. Although it is a short walk, we were often not eating until seven p.m. When other children her age were getting ready for bed, Allison was beginning her playtime with Mommy and Daddy. More often than not we would have her up until ten p.m. simply so that we could spend time with her. On some level we knew we shouldn't do it, because really she should have been going to bed at a more reasonable hour for her age. But to be honest, I think we selfishly craved time with her.

After all that stimulation, it was often difficult to get her to sleep—as you can imagine. Vince began trying to soothe her to bed, holding her and rocking her in his arms. She would cry and throw a fit if he put her down into her crib before she had completely fallen asleep. More often than not I would find the two of them asleep in the rocking chair in her room. My husband had turned into Allison's human security blanket.

It seemed that we made parenting error after parenting error and had created an awful situation. One night after Vince had put Allison to bed, he slowly and quietly made his way down the hall to the living room where I was sitting, ironically enough reading a parenting magazine.

Looking down, Vince put his hand through his hair and sat down on the sofa next to me.

"We've got to do something about this. We can't continue to keep her up this late. I also don't know how much longer I can continue to be her only way to get to sleep. There's no time left for anything at night except to go sleep ourselves because we both have to be at work early in the morning."

Touching his hand I said, "I know, I know we need to. Unfortunately I think we've created something of a monster."

Within a few months of that conversation, Allison turned two. As part of her birthday present we bought her a big-girl bed. I read somewhere that sometimes when you are having trouble transitioning your child toward independent sleeping, moving them to a toddler bed helps—the idea being that they are graduating to a big-kid item and therefore they don't need the crutch, in our case Vince's rocking, anymore.

The first night that Allison had the bed, she seemed really excited to be a big girl and sleep in it. We tucked her into bed around 8:30 p.m. and said our good-nights. Retreating back to our bedroom, we waited to see if it would work. Within five minutes we had our answer.

The door to Allison's room opened. A moment later, I saw the door to our room slowly open.

"Allison, why aren't you in bed?"

"Daddy."

"Sweetie, Daddy will tuck you in again but, you're a big girl now, and big girls sleep in their beds."

Vince shot me a look and, swooping Allison up in his arms, he again tucked her into bed.

Returning to our bedroom, Vince shook his head. "I don't think this is gonna work, Kate. I just don't."

Much to my dismay, he was right. For the next two hours we went back and forth putting Allison back in bed. Instead of motivating her to sleep, the bed without bars allowed her liberties beyond what she had known before—freedom she was now using to her advantage.

Now instead of having a daughter who wouldn't sleep and would cry in her room, we had one who, if she was displeased, simply walked out of her room and into ours. One night, I sat up and counted her getting out of her bed 150 times. It was like this most nights for three weeks.

Recognizing our mistake, we have tried, painfully tried, to rectify it. I have read books, watched shows, and researched on the Internet. All the books say it's never too late to change sleep habits, but they also say you can't expect quick results for behavior that has developed over years. We have not given up, and we are continuing to try to break her of this behavior by not giving in to her fits and calmly putting her back in her room.

Before I became a parent, I don't think I realized the importance of consistency and avoiding crutches. We didn't consistently follow through in setting and enforcing boundaries with Allison, and we further enabled her misbehavior by the use of Vince to pacify her. I believe we are on the right track now as we continue to try to alter the monster we created.

Be careful about patterns of enabling and lax discipline. What might be cute or bearable when they are very young will soon become awful as they age. Start early and be consistent. If you do make a mistake, don't be afraid to pick yourself up and correct the problem.

If Lost, Return to a
Childlike State

*Christy's Missing Pages: When you
can't find your child*

"AUSTIN?" I TURNED to my eight-year-old son, Robert. "Robert, where is Austin?" He shrugged and wrinkled his forehead in response.

Carrying Preston, my eighteen-month-old, on my hip, I had walked forward and completely lost sight of my three-year-old son, Austin. My eyes scanned the upper level in the foyer of the restaurant we were in. Throngs of people milled about, jockeying for a view of the horses. It was Mother's Day at Pimlico Race Track, and Austin seemed to have vanished into thin air.

Turning around, I called his name again. "Austin. Pleeeaasse Austin, come out. Mommy is worried!" This time my voice was an octave higher. My heart seemed to skip a beat and return at a much faster rate. Zac, my husband, turned back toward me from the hostess stand to see what was going on. The panic spread across my face made him, and his parents, rush toward me.

"Zac. I can't find Austin. I turned to come up the escalator and then he was gone. Have you seen him?"

"No, I haven't." Alarm spread on Zac's face and the faces of his parents.

My body began to shake with the nervous energy that was spreading through me. "I mean, what if he went back down the escalator and he's outside on the street?"

Before I finished my sentence, my husband and his parents were heading for the escalator toward the city street that was immediately outside it. Watching them descend on the escalator, I missed—yes, missed—the fact that Robert had now wandered off. Scanning the room, I found him in a side hallway, near the extra tables lined up for the brunch. I watched as he methodically looked under each one.

I heard laughter and saw Robert smile.

Underneath the long white tablecloth was Austin. Running over to him, I knelt and put Preston down on the floor. As Austin emerged, I pulled him toward me and hugged him. Still giggling, Austin didn't seem to understand my actions. Pushing him away from me, I put my hands on his shoulders and looked into his clear blue eyes.

"Austin! You can't ever run off like that again. Especially in a busy place like this! Mommy and Daddy were so scared you were lost!"

Austin's giggles immediately turned off as he realized that he had misbehaved. I hugged him again and stroked his mop of blond curls, simply grateful that I had him with me and he was not, as I feared, out on some city street. While doing so, I turned to Robert. "Robert, how on earth did you find Austin? How did you know where to look?"

With his hands tucked safely in his pockets, a wide smile on his face, Robert replied, "Easy, Mom. Sometimes you just gotta think like a kid."

Remember the child's perspective in life, especially in times of crisis. Sometimes it pays to "think like a kid."

Being the Second Mom

*Lisa's Missing Pages: When you are competing
with a biological parent*

"**I CAN'T BELIEVE** that you did this! I hate you and will never forgive you!" Jimmy, my sixteen-year-old stepson, yelled at me.

Alex, my biological son, who was also sixteen, stood between Jimmy and me in our kitchen.

"Jimmy! Mom did nothing wrong. I don't know what you're talking about. Really, man, where are you getting your information?"

I raised my right hand and looked down; I had no idea what was really at the root of this, but I'd had enough. I couldn't stand it anymore. Jimmy had never yelled at me like this before. Now he stood before me saying that I had done things that I hadn't. A relationship that took years to build was disintegrating in front of me, and I didn't understand why. I am not an overly emotional person, but this had pushed me over the edge. Before I knew it, I was uncontrollably crying.

"Dude! Really look at what you're doin' to Mom!" Alex said, gesturing toward me as if I were on display.

At that moment my husband, Bill, Jimmy's father, was drawn into the kitchen from the hall.

"What's going on, boys?" Bill said, but they completely ignored him.

Then he saw me standing slightly away from them, crying. Before he could ask me what had happened, Jimmy moved toward Alex until the two were within inches of each other.

"I don't care. She deserves it. She ruined my night!" Jimmy screamed.

At this point my husband stepped between Alex and Jimmy. Facing his son, he said through a clenched jaw, "Son, that's about enough." Pointing to me, he added, "If you can't respect her, you're not going to live here."

"Fine! I'm outta here." Jimmy sneered and left the room.

"Be careful about the choices you make, Jimmy," Bill hollered after him. Equally perplexed by his outburst, he came over and held me.

Exhausted, I sat in the kitchen, staring down the hallway and out the glass storm door. Within ten minutes, I watched Jimmy heading out that door to his girlfriend's mother's car. I openly stared at the door that had just shut. Light-headed and bewildered, I left the kitchen for the sanctuary of my bedroom and cried.

Before returning downstairs, I went into my bathroom. Taking a moment, I splashed cold water on my face, reddened by extended crying. The reflection in the mirror was jarring, almost as much as the interchange downstairs. Mentally flipping through recent events, I tried to make sense of what had provoked Jimmy. It didn't add up, and I couldn't understand how we had gotten here.

I inhaled deeply, straightened my shirt, and pushed my hair back behind my ears. The intensity of the situation and my response to it had surprised me. I turned and grabbed a fistful of tissues before returning downstairs—just in case I once again couldn't control the tears.

In the kitchen, I made myself a cup of chamomile tea and sat at the breakfast table. I wanted a moment to comprehend what had recently transpired. Over the last ten years I had built a strong relationship with Jimmy. We had experienced minor bumps, but nothing like today.

My husband won full parental custody of Jimmy when he was young—he's lived with us since he was six years old. When Bill assumed custody of Jimmy, it was during a period when Bill's ex-wife, Cheryl, Jimmy's mom, was living with another man and not doing well financially. Cheryl had maintained to Bill, and probably to Jimmy, that she would regain custody of him again when she was on her feet. She never did.

Throughout the years I have raised him with my own son, our bond close enough that he even refers to me as "Mom." Jimmy isn't, and has never really been, an overtly affectionate child, but I knew he loved me. When he was sick or needed to go to the doctor, I took him. If he was having trouble at school or with classwork, I counseled or tutored him. I was the one volunteering in the classroom or going on field trips. I was doing everything that a mother should—only I think that Jimmy wished it had been his own mother and not me.

Over the last ten years there were instances where he blamed me, but there had never been overt shouting. Although the teenage years were getting more challenging—probably because most teenagers blame their parents for everything anyway—Jimmy's behavior was different from my son Alex's, and they were the same age. It didn't make sense. The only thing I could attribute it to was that I wasn't his biological mom and he resented that

I was doing everything his own mom—in his mind—should be doing. On some level I think he felt rejected by her, a rejection reinforced every time there was a motherly duty that I performed in her stead.

It's painful to work hard to treat a child as if he is your own, to do everything for him, that his own mother won't do, and then to suddenly have the relationship thrown out the window because he's not getting his way. It killed me to think I had spent so many years trying to make a cohesive family, to have it destroyed in merely a few moments. What was perhaps more perplexing was that I had no idea why things had blown up to the level they had this time. Jimmy had stormed into the room, ranting and raving seemingly out of nowhere.

I sat Alex down with Bill and tried to piece together what exactly had happened. Thankfully Alex and Jimmy not only consider each other brothers but are the best of friends and run in the same circles.

"Mom. It's because of what you said about Cheryl and the party they were going to throw the kids," Alex explained.

My mind drifted back to when, a few weeks ago, Cheryl announced she was going to throw a co-ed sleepover party at her family's home in a neighboring county. I wasn't concerned they would give the teens drugs or alcohol or anything like that. I simply didn't think it appropriate to have a bunch of teenagers with raging hormones at a co-ed sleepover.

The party hadn't really come up again until yesterday, when one of the parents of a young woman invited to the sleepover called me to ask what I thought about it. The mother asked, "Would you throw a party like that?" I answered honestly, "No, I wouldn't."

"Alex, why is this such an issue? You and Jimmy both know I would never throw a party like that. That's all I said to Samantha's mom."

Alex looked down and then back at me. "But, Mom, didn't you also tell the other moms not to allow their kids to go?"

"Excuse me? No, I never told anyone not to go! Where did you, or he, get this information from?"

Shifting in his chair, Alex started to fidget. He was distinctly uncomfortable but knew he was going to have to finish telling all he knew.

"Mom, you told Samantha's mom, Kathy, they shouldn't go. Samantha told Jimmy what you said. She also said that her mom had talked to the other girls' moms and also told them what you said. So now no one is going."

Oh my gosh, this was getting worse by the moment. But I hadn't gotten to the worst of it yet.

Alex continued. "Well . . . Jimmy called Cheryl and told her that you were talking badly about her and her family to all of his friends. So now they're upset too."

I held my head in my hands, my elbows resting on the table. Not only had I not said any of these things, but now this untruth had been perpetuated to essentially my extended family, with whom relations were already tenuous. Well, it was time to start making this wrong right.

Picking up the phone, I called Kathy—the mother with whom I had originally spoken.

"Hey, Kathy, it's Lisa Massey, Jimmy and Alex's mom. Sorry to bother you with this, but we've had some confusion on our end and I am just trying to clear a few things up. Can you repeat to me what you recall hearing me say about Cheryl's co-ed sleepover party?"

"Sure, no problem. You said, 'It will probably be okay, but it's not something that I would do or allow in my home.' Is there a problem?"

I went on to detail all that happened and how this had turned into a rather ugly mess. Within minutes she had her daughter on the speakerphone and explained to her what had happened. It was then that Samantha added further clarification.

"Oh my gosh, Mrs. Massey. I feel horrible. This is all *my* fault. When my mom said that she asked you, 'If it were you, would you allow it?' and you said, 'No,' I thought she was asking your opinion on whether we should be allowed to go to the party. Not whether you would even *allow* a co-ed party. Then when she told me I couldn't go, I assumed it was because you said we shouldn't be allowed to. I then told everyone that you said we all shouldn't be allowed to go. I'm really sorry."

Her apology was much appreciated, but the damage was done. The issue wasn't really about the party anyway; Jimmy felt I had attacked his biological mother just when she was reaching out and trying to do something for him. No matter how much love I extended to Jimmy and no matter how much he loved me, he was always going defer to her. I could withhold my love from him, protect myself from heartache, but I knew that deep down I couldn't do that. Regardless of his feelings toward me, Jimmy is and always will be my son.

Later that week, while still at his girlfriend's house, Jimmy wrote me a note apologizing for his behavior. Unable to speak the words, he simply handed it to me. In return, I reached out, hugged him, and said, "I don't want you to be gone. I want you here as part of *this* family. But you need to really be here and be a part of *us*."

Jimmy did move back home a week later, but our relationship was never the same after that. In fact, I would say Jimmy and Alex's relationship also changed; much of the closeness that we had as a family vanished.

After that experience I tried to better understand my role for Jimmy. I had treated him much like my own son. But the reality is that he is not my biological son. As long as the biological mom is in the picture, you can be there, but expect to be in the background. No matter how strained the relationship is between a child and his mother, he will never want to betray his "real mom" by giving his whole heart to you.

Understand that if you play the role of stepparent, no matter how much you love the child it will always be a different relationship than that of the child and their biological parent. Be prepared to take second place and do what you can to work with your stepchild to create the best possible relationship at that level.

It Was All Worth It

*Matt's Missing Pages: When becoming
a parent isn't as easy as expected*

WHEN MY WIFE, Delphine, began trying to get pregnant, I remember being nervous about becoming a parent. All I thought about was the amount of responsibility and hard work. I honestly thought about how it would take away time from other things I could be doing. I thought about Delphine's career that she loved and how it could impact her. Although we wanted kids, there was a certain anxiety about how they would also negatively impact our lives. I think we took for granted that we would have a kid, buy a house, and live our lives.

Then she couldn't get pregnant.

Faced with infertility issues, over the next eight years we went through multiple cycles of fertility treatments, three surgeries, and one miscarriage. Amid all of this we often received comments or questions such as, "Why don't you have kids yet?" or "You're not getting any younger." To that I just wanted to say, "Shut up." I didn't, however, because we didn't want our infertility on display.

Even the casual observation, "You guys would make great parents," was hurtful. Sometimes I responded to it with, "Thank you, we think so too," and then later, when I couldn't deflect anymore, I became honest and responded with, "Yeah, we've been trying for a lot of years now." The pained reaction I would get in return made me feel—even if only for a moment—that the person asking finally felt some of my torment. But revealing our infertility had its own issues as well.

The minute that someone finds out that you are having a hard time having kids, they launch into a story. They know somebody . . . somebody who stopped trying and had a kid. Or maybe it was their dental hygienist's sister in-law's cousin—or someone equally removed—who was in the same situation and then adopted a dog and became pregnant. The stories are well-intentioned, but instead of making you feel better they are just one more reminder of another couple, perhaps one just like you, who have had a successful pregnancy when you have not.

We were running out of options, and Delphine was getting older. The last frontier that we had not pursued yet was IVF. The decision to pursue IVF was huge. Through our infertility journey we endured a number of procedures, each more expensive than the last one. We knew that we could pursue IVF, spend all the money we had set aside for a house, and fail. There was a chance that we wouldn't be successful, but we also knew if we didn't try there would be little to no possibility that Delphine would ever get pregnant. Coming this far, we couldn't bear to turn back without trying. If there was a chance we could become parents, then it was worth the financial risk and potential emotional roller coaster. We wanted to be parents, *badly*.

Committed to IVF, we were hopeful going into our first cycle of it. Everything was going well until right before the egg retrieval. For an unknown reason, Delphine's estrogen levels skyrocketed and the entire cycle had to be abandoned. It was yet another devastating blow, and we returned to square one.

The second cycle of IVF was successful. They were able to retrieve twelve eggs. Of these twelve, eight matured, five were successfully fertilized, and ultimately two embryos were implanted. When they told us that Delphine was pregnant with twins, my mouth went dry and there was a rush of adrenaline. Maybe this time it would work.

Given the previous miscarriage, I tried to contain my excitement. However, as the pregnancy successfully progressed, my confidence and elation grew and we began to share the news of the pregnancy with others.

The responses to our good news were often surprising. Instead of, "Wow that's great!" I received things like, "Twins, aw man . . . you're screwed," or they would look at me and my pregnant wife and say, "Enjoy your freedom now." It was as if there was an evil villain lurking in the background, his voice echoing in the darkness: "Ha, ha, ha . . . welcome to the club that sucks—parenthood."

After everything we had gone through to get to this point, it seemed hard to believe that being a parent would be as awful as other parents were making it out to be. But based on all the comments we received, we were beginning to wonder. You hear all of these negative things about how hard it is, and instead of being excited, irrational worries set in. Eventually for us we concluded, hard or not, this was what we wanted. This was what we chose, so we'd just have to suck it up and move forward. This negativity lurked in the background during what otherwise was a very exciting time in our lives.

That negativity was short-lived.

Delphine gave birth to Abigail and Zachary via C-section. I remember the initial moment when they pulled Abigail from Delphine. In that instant, all I saw was this perfect little girl, and all I kept saying was, "Wow." I had an image in my mind as to what my kids were going to look like, but the reality of Abigail was far beyond what I envisioned. Then Zachary was born.

As they pulled my son out of Delphine and introduced him to me, my heart raced and a grin spread across my face. Looking at my son was like looking at my baby picture. After all of these years of waiting, I had not one, but two children—a daughter *and* a son.

I realized in that moment, through all of those procedures and all of the years of failure, I had begun to love my yet-to-be-born children. It was that love, I think, that carried us through those darker times. Why else would anyone put themselves through all of that heartache?

Holding my children to me, playing with their small fingers and feeling their tiny heartbeats, spread warmth throughout me. Parts of me awakened for the first time. I was in love in a way different from anything I'd ever known. Nothing was, or is, as important as them. I couldn't believe how different I felt, now that they were here. I also couldn't believe people don't emphasize how amazing it is. How joyous it is to be a parent—to be a part of another being's life in a way unlike any other.

Our first night in the hospital after they were born, Delphine was finally strong enough to hold one of our children. As she held one, I held the other, and we simply sat there looking at the miracles in our arms.

Turning toward her, I said, "It was all worth it."

"You're right," she said. "It *was* all worth it."

Sometimes the journey to becoming a parent is longer than we expect and fraught with challenges. Whatever path you choose, whether it be to seek assistance with fertility issues or through adoption, the hard work will pay off. If you really want to be a parent, then hang in there— it really is all worth it.

Missing Pages

Your Missing Pages: When . . .

DO YOU HAVE MISSING PAGES that you want to share? I would love to hear your parenting experiences because I truly believe that we can all learn from one another and take comfort in knowing that we are not all alone in this parenting journey. Please visit www.christinabrockett.com and let me know your story.

Afterword

RECENTLY I WAS SITTING with a group of my girlfriends, who are also moms, and we were discussing my experience writing this book. I shared with them the incredible journey I had while writing it. While we chatted over a glass of wine, one asked, "So, did you learn anything?" I learned a lot of things, but I shared the following story with them.

Late last winter, my children were driving me crazy. My son had just turned ten and my daughter was six. Time-outs weren't working—*nothing* was working. Sometimes I'd find myself, arms crossed and lips pressed together, in standoffs with my six-year-old daughter. It wasn't productive—for either of us. Then I remembered Emily's story of the ticket system.

I had my husband, Tom, read the story and talked to him about implementing a ticket system in our house. Having come home on multiple occasions with me ready to run out the door and to a neighbor's house for a break from the kids, he was willing to give it a try. If it would stop the madness, then he was for it.

In our house the tickets were made from scrapbooking paper, affixed to thin magnets and placed on a magnetic whiteboard next to which hangs our Brockett House Rules—rules that were developed with the kids. We followed Emily's story's suggestion that you start with seven tickets at the beginning of the week. If you break a rule, you lose a ticket. If you do something without being asked—we actually now have a list of suggested activities in our house—then you can earn one. If you drop below seven, you lose a privilege; if you have more than ten, you get a prize. The system empowers my kids to be in control of their behavior and their destinies. I also like that it encourages them to think outside themselves, so they look for ways to help out without being asked.

Initially it worked like a charm, especially for my six-year-old daughter. But my son soon figured out how to work the system to his advantage. Of the two children, my son rarely violated the rules. For him it was easy to coast and not lose tickets. This was great in some ways, but it defeated part of the lesson we were trying to teach—that there is an obligation to help others. As a result, we made a modification.

Now our kids have to earn minimum of two tickets a week. If they fail to do so, they will lose a ticket. If they haven't lost any other tickets, then they are only one good deed away from a prize. If they have lost a bunch of tickets, they still have the consequence of losing a privilege. Nine months later, the system is working well. When we went on vacation to Disney World and the beach, we took a picture of the house rules with our cell phones so that we could reference it while away. Ironically, the other families on these vacations with us also began adopting the same process—seeing how well and easily it worked with our kids.

Through the course of putting this book together, I have gathered many pages my parent handbook didn't have—and just as many I didn't even know existed. Some of the lessons I actively incorporate or reflect on when certain situations arise—such as staying calm in the face of upset or focusing on redirecting. Other lessons I hope I never have to face—such as losing a parent or a child—but even within these I feel I can use some elements of what those parents shared, such as living life in the present, and really being there for my kids.

Perhaps my biggest takeaway from this experience is that as parents, we have a responsibility to parent with both our hearts and minds. We need to raise healthy, happy, and self-sustaining children. Equally important is that we are the face of compassion and understanding for our misunderstood children—or even for those who are only slightly outside the mainstream. Whether a child has a medical condition, mental health issues, or a different sexual orientation, or merely dresses differently, we as parents need to focus on putting aside our preconceived notions, offer our children unconditional love, and seek to understand who they really are. If our children can't expect unconditional love from us, where will they ever find it?

Until next time, try to enjoy *your* wild parenting ride.

Acknowledgments

My two monkeys, being your mother has taught me how little I really know. I have learned to be a better person and grown immeasurably since having you. I love you both more than all the stars in the universe.

Tom Brockett, my rock and the love of my life.

All the parents, those whose stories appear in these pages and those whose aren't, who shared their homes, hearts, and stories with me; without their generosity this book would not have been possible.

Catheryn Brockett, my writing sister. Your brilliant insight and insistence freed boundaries.

Jennifer Graham, my sister. Thank you for always pushing me to pursue things close to my heart.

David Hazard, my mentor. You saw the need for this to become a book even before I did and kept reading, pen poised, as it slowly came together.

Ally Machate, my editor. Talented beyond measure.

Suzanne and Pat Reynolds, George Norton and April Dyett, my parents and stepparents. The rocky roads and your love have taught me a lot. I would not be the parent I am today without these experiences. Mom, thanks for your input and for listening, even if you didn't always understand my challenges with the book. Dad, I was glad to work with you on this, even if it was sometimes just an excuse to be together and talk. April, what can I say? Your innate wisdom as a writer and vision are amazing.

Warren and Dorothy Brockett, my in-laws and outstanding parents. Tom emulates you with our children, and through this I have learned volumes.

Heather Haberle, Molly and Paul Brockett. Great friends, great family, and great support.

My *Little Indians*: Jackie Flynn, Sharon Lang, Emily Freund, Shaney Nadel, Sandy Cadwell, Colleen Casaus, Chris Kenney and Elaine Rosen. Thanks for supporting me as a friend, a mother and in writing this book. Here's to the next thirty years of friendship.